Make Disciples, Not Followers:
A Biblical Guide to Christian Online Witness

By: Rev. Benjamin J. Stern

Copyright

Make Disciples, Not Followers:
A Biblical Guide to Christian Online Witness

© 2025 by Reverend Benjamin J. Stern

All rights reserved.

No part of this publication may be reproduced, stored in a retrieval system, or transmitted in any form or by any means — electronic, mechanical, photocopying, recording, or otherwise — without the prior written permission of the publisher, except in the case of brief quotations in critical articles or reviews.

Scripture Acknowledgment

Scripture quotations, unless otherwise indicated, are from the Revised Standard Version of the Bible,

Copyright © 1952 [2nd edition, 1971] by the Division of Christian Education of the National Council of Churches of Christ in the U.S.A.

Used by permission. All rights reserved.

Disclaimer: This work represents the author's theological and pastoral reflections and does not necessarily reflect the official positions of any ecclesiastical jurisdiction or organization.

Dedication

To all who share the Gospel with humility and courage—who speak truthfully, love their neighbor, refuse contempt, and embody the best the Christian tradition has to offer.

And with particular gratitude to **Austin Suggs** (*Gospel Simplicity*) and **Gavin Ortlund** (*Truth Unites*): brothers in Christ from traditions other than my own, whose clarity, charity, and reverence have helped me grow, deepen my appreciation for the wider Church, and listen more faithfully. May many who labor online and offline learn to imitate what is best in their witness, so that Jesus Christ may increase.

Table of Contents

Introduction

    Introduction — The Temptation of the Platform (and the Call of Christ)...Page 6

Part I — The Call and the Measure

    1. Why Online Influence and Evangelism? ....Page 14

    2. The Measure of Faithfulness: Fruit, Not Virality .... Page 24

Part II — The Messenger Must Be Formed

    3. A Rule of Life for Digital Mission .... Page 33

    4. Begin With Self-Conversion: The Beam and the Speck ....Page 38

    5. Weakness, Reluctance, and Calling: Power Made Perfect ....Page 44

    6. "He Must Increase, I Must Decrease": Escaping the Cult of Personality... 51

Part III — Truth, Fairness, and Speech

    7. Know the Truth—Because God Is the Author of Truth ....Page 58

    8. Controversy, Straw Men, and the Duty of Fairness ....Page 65

    9. We Stand Under Judgment: The Person Behind the Screen ....Page 72

    10. Speech That Heals: Rebuke Without Contempt .... Page 79

    11. Prayer as the Engine of Theology: Doxology First .... Page 86

Part IV — Stewardship, Authority, and Holy Reserve

    12. Under Authority: Correction, Accountability, and Communion ...... Page 92

    13. Stewards of Mysteries: Reverence, Reserve, and "Pearls" ....Page 100

    14. Enduring Criticism and Hardship: Prophets, Apostles, and Comment Sections .... Page 108

15. Vocation or Job? Money, Patronage, and the Burden on the Church ...Pg 116

Part V — Embodied Witness and the Public Square

16. Authentic Faith: Light in the World, Not Merely Winning Arguments .. Pg 124
17. No Christianity Based on Hate: Creation, Neighbor, and the Image of God ....Page 131
18. The Online Church and the Parish Church: ....Page 138
19. Prophetic Voices Online ....Page 146
20. Conversions and Responsibility: ....Page 153

Conclusion

- The Demand of Discipleship in the Age of Cheap Grace ....Pg 160

Appendices

- Appendix A — Discernment Worksheet: "Should I Post This?"
- Appendix B — Code of Ethics for Christian Content Creators

Introduction

The Temptation of the Platform (and the Call of Christ)

The Church has always proclaimed the Gospel in the languages, media, and public spaces of its day. The apostles preached in synagogues and marketplaces, wrote letters that circulated from city to city, and trusted that the Spirit could carry the message farther than their own voices. Today, the "marketplace" is often a screen, and the "letters" are posts, videos, threads, livestreams, podcasts, and comments that can travel across the world in seconds. That is not inherently a problem. In many ways, it is a providential opening. A person who would never walk into a church can quietly listen to Scripture, hear a testimony, encounter a thoughtful defense of the faith, or see a life shaped by Christ. The missionary horizon is real.

But so is the temptation.

The modern platform is not a neutral instrument. It is built to capture attention, to keep eyes and thumbs moving, to turn human curiosity into measurable engagement. It rewards what provokes quick emotion—especially outrage, fear, mockery, and tribal belonging. It trains creators (often without their realizing it) to speak faster than they can think, to respond before they can pray, to publish before they can verify, and to interpret people as audiences rather than neighbors. Even Christian content can be pulled into this machinery until it becomes "spiritual entertainment": inspirational clips, constant hot takes, and endless conflict dressed up as discernment. Sometimes it looks like zeal. Sometimes it feels like courage. Yet it can quietly detach the messenger from the message, and the message from the Lord.

This book is written for Christians who sense both realities: that online evangelism can be a genuine work of mercy, and that online influence can also become a spiritual danger—especially when it begins to shape our souls more than the Gospel does.

The call: disciples, not followers

The risen Christ did not command the apostles to gather attention. He commanded them to make disciples. "Go therefore and make disciples of all nations... teaching them to observe all that I have commanded you" (Matthew 28:19–20, RSV). That word—*disciple*—matters. A disciple is not a consumer of religious content, not a subscriber, not a "like," not a member of a fandom. A disciple is a learner and follower, formed by obedience, drawn into communion with God, and sent to love and serve. When the Great Commission becomes a strategy for building a platform, the goal quietly shifts from obedience to influence. The platform becomes the center; Christ becomes a theme.

Online Christian influencing is therefore never justified merely because it is effective. The question is not, "Did it go viral?" but, "Did it produce discipleship—repentance, faith, worship, love of neighbor, and perseverance in the way of Christ?" A post can win an argument and still lose a person. A video can gain a thousand followers and still fail to teach obedience. If the Church remembers what Christ actually said, many of our online pathologies begin to loosen their grip.

The temptation: being conformed to the age

Saint Paul describes the basic spiritual pressure every age exerts: "Do not be conformed to this world but be transformed by the renewal of your mind" (Romans 12:2, RSV). Social platforms specialize in conformity. They form habits of mind: outrage as reflex, suspicion as default, speed over wisdom, branding over integrity, performative certainty over humble truth-seeking. When Christians spend hours in these environments, it is not only that we *use* the platform; the platform begins to *use* us—shaping what we desire, what we fear, how we speak, and what we believe success looks like.

This conformity can appear in obvious ways: cruelty in comment sections, contempt for "the other side," and the ease of calling people fools. But it can also appear in subtler ways: the temptation to speak beyond our knowledge, to repeat rumors because they fit a narrative, to publish "quick takes" without verification, to dramatize conflict because drama boosts engagement. A Christian creator can sincerely love Christ and still be trained by the algorithm into habits that contradict Christ.

Paul's command is not withdrawal from public life. It is a different kind of presence: transformed, renewed, and able to "prove what is the will of God, what is good and acceptable and perfect" (Romans 12:2). The world will always want to catechize us into its instincts. A Christian evangelist must resist being shaped by the very environment in which he or she speaks.

Earthen vessels and the danger of self-display

One of the most searching passages for online ministry is Paul's description of apostolic proclamation: "For what we preach is not ourselves, but Jesus Christ as Lord, with ourselves as your servants for Jesus' sake" (2 Corinthians 4:5, RSV). Platforms reward "preaching ourselves"—even when we use the name of Jesus. They encourage a personality-driven economy: brands, identities, factions, and loyalty to a particular voice. It is dangerously easy for Christian content to become a form of self-display: *my* discernment, *my* courage, *my* certainty, *my* righteousness, *my* audience.

Paul immediately grounds the minister in humility: "We have this treasure in earthen vessels, to show that the transcendent power belongs to God and not to us" (2 Corinthians 4:7). Online influence magnifies the vessel. The Gospel tells us to magnify the treasure. The goal of Christian online witness is not to make the vessel impressive, but to make Christ visible—so that any good accomplished is clearly attributable to God's power, not our charisma.

This is why the Christian influencer must first be a Christian: a person under discipline, under prayer, under correction, under the ordinary means of grace, and under the costly command to love. Without that, the platform becomes a spiritual amplifier of the self, and the "content" becomes increasingly detached from holiness.

A real missionary opportunity—if we refuse the devil's bargain

None of this is meant to shame sincere evangelists, catechists, apologists, or Christian educators online. Many are doing holy work. Many have helped people return to prayer, Scripture, and the sacraments; many have encouraged the lonely and defended the vulnerable; many have offered clarity amid confusion. The missionary opportunity is real. The question is whether we will seize that opportunity on Christ's terms, or on the platform's terms.

The platform offers a bargain: speak in the way that wins, not in the way that heals. Keep people angry so they stay engaged. Reduce complex persons to enemies. Turn theology into entertainment. Replace patience with speed. Replace charity with sarcasm. Replace conversion with applause.

Christ offers a different way: speak the truth in love, suffer misunderstanding, remain faithful, and entrust results to God.

This book is written to help readers refuse the devil's bargain.

What this book will do

This is a biblical guide to online influencing and evangelism. It is not a technical manual for growing an audience. It is not a marketing blueprint. It is not a promise of "success." It is a call to discipleship for those who speak in public. It will argue, from Scripture, that Christian online witness must be rooted in:

- **Self-conversion and humility**, lest we denounce others while ignoring our own sin.

- **Truthfulness**, including careful verification—refusing rumors, misinformation, and reckless "quick takes."

- **Charity in argument**, including a rejection of straw men and the commitment to represent others fairly.

- **Pastoral sensitivity**, recognizing that content can "win" and still wound—causing scandal, despair, or unnecessary division.

- **Boundaries and privacy**, because people are not content, and because spiritual counsel cannot be reduced to DMs and social media dependence.

- **Prayer and accountability**, because theology must return to worship and evangelists must accept correction.

- **The costly way of the cross**, because discipleship cannot be traded for cheap grace and likes.

Each chapter will also name a recurring reality: **the platform temptation**. You will see, again and again, how the incentives of online systems subtly pressure Christians toward habits contrary to Christ—and how Scripture forms a different set of instincts.

A first platform temptation: speed without truth

To begin, consider one temptation that will recur throughout the book: speed. Platforms reward immediacy. They reward the first reaction, the fastest clip, the quickest accusation. But Scripture calls Christians to truthfulness, patience, and careful speech. "Let every man be quick to hear, slow to speak, slow to anger" (James 1:19, RSV). The moral cost of being wrong online is often carried by someone else: the person slandered, the community misrepresented, the fragile believer confused, the outsider confirmed in cynicism.

Verification is not optional for Christians. To repeat an unverified claim because it helps "our side" is to love tribal victory more than truth. And if God is the author of all truth, then contempt for truth is contempt for God. The evangelical harm is direct: when Christians are careless with facts, unbelievers conclude that Christianity is careless with reality.

This book will insist on a discipline that feels almost foreign in the attention economy: **stop, verify, pray, and then speak—or choose silence.**

A second platform temptation: winning that wounds

Another recurring temptation is the thrill of the "win." A cutting line, a humiliating takedown, a viral clapback can feel like righteousness—especially when the target is genuinely wrong. But the Gospel does not authorize contempt. The Christian can denounce sin and still refuse cruelty. Jesus convicted without becoming a performer of disdain; he told stories that exposed hearts, not merely slogans that inflamed crowds.

Pastoral sensitivity matters because the audience is never only "them." It includes the scrupulous, the wounded, the traumatized, the spiritually immature, and the seeker peering through the window. Content that escalates hostility may energize the already-convinced, while hardening the skeptic and crushing the weak. Paul's words should haunt Christian creators: "For what we preach is not ourselves... but Jesus Christ as Lord" (2 Corinthians 4:5). If our style makes Christ seem petty, cruel, or tribal, we have not preached Christ well—even if our propositions were correct.

A third platform temptation: intimacy without responsibility

Finally, platforms blur boundaries. People confess in comment sections. They disclose trauma in DMs. They cling to creators as substitutes for community, spiritual fathers or mothers they have never met. Some creators invite this dependence because it increases engagement and loyalty. Others fall into it out of compassion, not realizing the moral responsibilities they are assuming.

But the Christian must remember: people are not content. Families are not props. Minors must be protected. Private struggles should not be leveraged for public branding. And spiritual counsel belongs within the Church's careful forms of accountability and pastoral care, not in improvised, confidential chat threads where no one can safeguard either the vulnerable person or the counselor.

Boundaries are not a lack of love. They are a form of love.

The aim: faithful witness in a hostile and hungry world

We live in a time when many are hostile to Christianity, and many are hungry for God. The same person can be both. Some have been wounded by churches, manipulated by ideologues, exhausted by culture wars, and numbed by entertainment. Yet they still ache for meaning, forgiveness, belonging, and hope. The online world is often where that ache is first expressed.

The call of Christ remains: go, teach, baptize, form disciples, and trust his presence: "Lo, I am with you always, to the close of the age" (Matthew 28:20). Online evangelism is one arena where that promise must be believed. The Lord is present not only in churches but in kitchens, dorm rooms, and late-night scrolling—wherever a person can hear and respond.

The question is whether those who speak of Christ online will do so as servants, or as celebrities; as witnesses, or as warriors; as disciples making disciples, or as brands gathering fans.

This book is an invitation to choose the harder path: the way of truth, prayer, humility, and love—the way of the cross—so that Christ may increase, and we may decrease.

Chapter 1

Why Online Influence and Evangelism?

The question is no longer whether people live online. They do. The question is whether Christians will meet them there as disciples of Jesus Christ—or whether we will enter the digital world on the world's terms, chasing attention, shaping our message to please crowds, and confusing influence with faithfulness. The Church's mission did not begin with platforms, and it will not end with platforms. But the platforms of this age have become a primary public square, and in that square the Church must decide what it means to speak in the name of Christ.

This chapter argues a simple claim: online influence and evangelism can be a genuine work of Christian mission, but only if the goal is discipleship rather than popularity. The Lord Jesus does not call the Church to gather "followers" in the modern sense. He calls the Church to make disciples—people who learn him, obey him, and take up his life as their own. When the goal is discipleship, a thousand distortions fall away. When the goal becomes likes, subscriptions, and applause, even sincere Christian witness can turn into something else.

The Commission: authority, mission, and presence

After the resurrection, Jesus speaks with the calm clarity of a King who has already won: "All authority in heaven and on earth has been given to me. Go therefore and make disciples of all nations, baptizing them… teaching them to observe all that I have commanded you" (Matthew 28:18–20, RSV). Notice what is emphasized.

First, the mission is grounded in Christ's authority, not ours. Online culture tempts us to build personal authority—brand credibility, influence, a loyal audience. The Great Commission begins by stripping that illusion away. The Church does not evangelize because it has seized a microphone; it evangelizes because Jesus reigns.

Second, the mission is defined as making disciples, not gathering crowds. The verb is not "attract," "entertain," or "go viral." It is "make disciples"—and Jesus specifies the means: baptism into the Triune Name, and teaching that leads to obedience. In other words, the Church is sent to form persons into a way of life, not to win momentary reactions.

Third, Jesus promises his presence: "Lo, I am with you always, to the close of the age" (Matthew 28:20). That promise matters for online ministry because much of it feels lonely and intangible. You may never see the fruit. You may not know who is listening. Yet Christ is present where his Gospel is proclaimed in truth and love, and where people are called into faithful obedience.

Mark records the same missionary impulse in compressed form: "Go into all the world and preach the gospel to the whole creation" (Mark 16:15). "All the world" includes the places people actually inhabit. In the first century, that meant roads, homes, synagogues, ports, and marketplaces. In the twenty-first century, it also includes feeds, search results, comment sections, group chats, livestreams, and long-form conversations that stretch late into the night. Christians are not required to be everywhere, but the Church is required to go where people are—especially where they are confused, lonely, spiritually hungry, or cut off from ordinary sources of help.

Acts makes the scope and power of the mission unmistakable: "You shall receive power when the Holy Spirit has come upon you; and you shall be my witnesses… to the end of the earth" (Acts 1:8, RSV). Online environments can help that outward movement, because they collapse distance. A person can hear a witness from across the globe. A seeker can encounter Scripture while sitting in a hospital room. A doubter can ask questions anonymously without fear. A lapsed Christian can begin again quietly. These are not small mercies. They are openings for grace.

But to speak about online mission biblically, we must be careful with our words—especially the words *influence* and *evangelism*.

Influence is not the Gospel, and the Gospel is not influence

In our era, "influence" often means the ability to shape opinions, preferences, and behavior through repeated exposure and perceived credibility. That can be used for good or ill. Influence itself is morally neutral; what matters is what it is ordered toward and what methods it uses.

Christian mission does not begin with influence. It begins with the Gospel: the good news of what God has done in Jesus Christ for the salvation of the world, and the call to repent, believe, be baptized, and follow him. Christian witness may produce influence as a byproduct, but influence is never the measure of fidelity. The Gospel often looks weak before it looks powerful. It is "treasure in earthen vessels" (2 Corinthians 4:7). The cross does not trend.

This is why Christian online work must begin by answering a diagnostic question: *What do I actually want?* Do I want to be known, or do I want Christ to be known? Do I want to win, or do I want people to be saved? Do I want to gather admirers, or do I want to form disciples who obey Jesus even when it costs them?

The New Testament does not flatter the Church with promises of constant public success. It promises faithfulness, suffering, joy, and the steady work of the Spirit. Online work becomes spiritually dangerous when a person starts to treat attention as proof of God's blessing and obscurity as failure. Jesus says, in effect, that the proof of discipleship is obedience: "teaching them to observe all that I have commanded you" (Matthew 28:20). A post can be widely praised and still produce no obedience. A small conversation can be forgotten by the world and remembered in eternity.

The platform temptation in this chapter: measuring the wrong thing

The earliest temptation for anyone doing online ministry is to measure success by the platform's metrics: likes, shares, watch time, downloads, subscriber count, comments, and engagement. Those are not worthless; they can indicate reach. But they are spiritually unreliable. A platform's metrics are designed to measure attention, not conversion; stimulation, not sanctification; reaction, not repentance.

If you consistently measure your ministry by applause, you will gradually edit your message and your methods to keep the applause coming. You will be tempted to speak more aggressively, to post more frequently, to oversimplify complex issues into "dunks," and to treat controversy as fuel. And even if you avoid obvious scandals, the subtle change is this: you will stop asking whether your work is producing disciples, and start asking whether it is producing engagement.

A Christian must resist that formation. The goal is not to gather an audience. The goal is to witness to Christ in such a way that people can respond with faith and be drawn into a life of discipleship.

To do that, we need clarity about what kinds of Christian speech we are actually doing online.

Five forms of Christian online ministry

Online Christian communication can take several distinct forms. Confusing them causes frustration and harm. A person might expect pastoral care from an apologetics channel, or treat testimony like a theological argument, or demand evangelistic simplicity from catechesis meant for the already-baptized. Each has its proper aim, tone, and responsibility.

1) Evangelism

Evangelism is proclaiming the Gospel to those who do not yet believe, or who have fallen away, with a genuine invitation to repentance and faith. It is not primarily about winning debates. It is about announcing Christ: who he is, what he has done, and what he commands.

Online evangelism often happens through:

- simple proclamation (short videos, posts, articles),
- answering basic questions of seekers,
- telling the story of salvation,
- inviting concrete next steps: prayer, Scripture, local Christian community, baptism, confession, reconciliation.

A key mark of evangelism is that it is outward-facing. It expects that many listeners are unfamiliar with Christian terms and may have past wounds. It speaks clearly, patiently, and without assuming insider knowledge.

Governing texts: Matthew 28:18–20; Mark 16:15; Acts 1:8.

2) Catechesis

Catechesis is instruction in the faith for those who are becoming Christians or seeking deeper formation—teaching that builds a coherent Christian mind and a practiced Christian life. It belongs to discipleship: "teaching them to observe all that I have commanded you" (Matthew 28:20).

Online catechesis can be excellent: systematic series, guided Bible study, introductions to creed and sacrament, moral formation, prayer training. But it must remain connected to embodied Christian community, because discipleship is not merely information transfer. The danger is that catechesis becomes disembodied intellectualism—learning without obedience, content without communion.

Catechesis must therefore be ordered toward real practices: prayer, worship, works of mercy, reconciliation, accountability, and life together.

3) Apologetics

Apologetics is reasoned defense and explanation of the faith, responding to objections and misunderstandings. It has an important place online, because the internet is full of arguments against Christianity and caricatures of Christian belief.

But apologetics is not evangelism, and it is not a substitute for holiness. A person can be brilliant and unconverted. A person can refute objections and still not love. Apologetics becomes spiritually dangerous when it turns into sport—argument for entertainment, debate for dominance, "owning" opponents for applause.

Healthy apologetics:

- aims at clarity, not humiliation,
- treats opponents as persons, not trophies,

- seeks truth rather than tribal victory,
- remembers that conversion is the Spirit's work, not a rhetorical trick.

4) Testimony

Testimony is the truthful telling of what God has done—how a person encountered Christ, repented, was healed, was carried through suffering, or found faith amid doubt. Testimony is powerful online because it speaks in the first person and can reach people who are not ready for formal argument.

But testimony carries responsibilities:

- it must be truthful (no embellishment for engagement),
- it must be humble (not centered on the self as hero),
- it must be discerning (not oversharing what should remain private),
- it must avoid presenting one person's experience as the universal pattern.

Testimony is not proof in the strict sense, but it can be a genuine witness: "You shall be my witnesses" (Acts 1:8).

5) Pastoral care online

Pastoral care is helping persons carry burdens, seek repentance, receive comfort, and walk toward healing and obedience. Online environments create real opportunities for pastoral care—especially for the isolated. Yet online care has strict limits.

Pastoral care online should be:

- gentle, prayerful, and cautious,
- clear about boundaries,

- oriented toward connecting people with real local support and accountable ministry,
- careful not to mimic sacramental confession or clinical therapy through informal messaging.

Some conversations should not happen in public comments. Some should not happen in DMs at all. Some require referral—because the soul is precious, and careless counsel can wound.

Discipleship as the integrating center

These five modes overlap, but discipleship must integrate them. Evangelism is the invitation into discipleship. Catechesis forms disciples. Apologetics protects disciples from confusion and answers honest questions. Testimony encourages disciples with hope. Pastoral care strengthens disciples when they stumble, suffer, or need guidance.

That is why the Great Commission is the anchor for every Christian who communicates online: "make disciples... teaching them to observe" (Matthew 28:19–20). A Christian creator should periodically ask:

- Am I teaching obedience—or only generating reactions?
- Do I invite people toward prayer, repentance, and community—or only toward my content?
- Do I leave people more charitable, more truthful, more humble—or more angry and tribal?
- Does my work point beyond me to Christ, or does it quietly orbit my personality?

The platform will not ask these questions. Christ does.

Practical aims for online evangelism that serve discipleship

If the goal is discipleship, online evangelism can take on clear and realistic aims. You are not required to "do everything." But you can be faithful in your lane. Here are aims that align with Scripture:

1. **Make Christ intelligible** to people who know only caricatures.
2. **Make Scripture accessible** through faithful reading and explanation.
3. **Make repentance imaginable** by speaking of sin without contempt and of mercy without sentimentality.
4. **Make next steps concrete**: prayer, a Gospel reading plan, a local church visit, speaking with a pastor, seeking baptism, seeking reconciliation.
5. **Make discipleship visible** by modeling a credible Christian life rather than a permanent online argument.

Witness "to the end of the earth" (Acts 1:8) is not only geographic. It includes social distance—the distant neighbor who would never otherwise hear a Christian speak without being mocked or threatened.

Chapter practices

A discipleship practice

Write a one-sentence mission statement for your online work that you can pray daily. For example:
"Lord Jesus Christ, let my words serve your Great Commission: not to gather admirers, but to make disciples who obey you."

A truthfulness practice

Before posting anything factual, adopt a simple rule: verify with at least two reliable sources, or do not post it as fact. If you cannot verify, say so—or stay silent.

Reflection questions

1. Which mode do you primarily operate in online (evangelism, catechesis, apologetics, testimony, pastoral care)? Are you accidentally doing a different mode than your audience expects?

2. What do you feel most strongly after posting: peace and prayerfulness, or adrenaline and craving for reaction? What might that reveal?

3. In what ways might your content be forming people into "followers" of you rather than disciples of Jesus?

4. What concrete next step do you regularly offer people—beyond watching your next video?

Closing prayer

Lord Jesus Christ, who has all authority in heaven and on earth, purify my motives and renew my mind. Make me your servant for your sake, that I may be your witness with truth and love. Draw those who hear into repentance, faith, and obedience, and keep me faithful to the end. Amen.

Chapter 2

The Measure of Faithfulness: Fruit, Not Virality

If you create Christian content online, you will eventually face a temptation that sounds reasonable and even "practical": *Surely the biggest numbers mean the biggest impact.* Platforms encourage that belief at every turn. They place metrics on your dashboard like a scoreboard—views, likes, shares, comments, subscriber count, watch time, impressions. They reward what keeps people engaged, and they penalize what people skip. Over time, these measurements can become a kind of catechism. Without noticing, you begin to learn what the platform "blesses," and you begin to think that blessing is the same as faithfulness.

But Christ measures differently.

In the Gospel of John, Jesus does not describe his disciples as brands competing for visibility. He describes them as branches that either bear fruit or wither. "I am the vine, you are the branches. He who abides in me, and I in him, he it is that bears much fruit, for apart from me you can do nothing" (John 15:5, RSV). The center of Christian mission is not performance but communion: abiding in Christ, receiving life from him, and bearing fruit that comes from that life.

The question that matters most for Christian online influence is therefore not, *Is this getting attention?* but, *Is this bearing fruit?* And the fruit Christ seeks is not merely the spread of information but the transformation of persons into disciples—people who abide, obey, love, endure, and become holy.

This chapter offers a biblical framework for evaluating online ministry so that you do not confuse virality with faithfulness, or visibility with spiritual fruit.

The platform temptation in this chapter: worshiping the dashboard

The dashboard is not evil. Numbers can help you understand whether people are finding your work, what topics confuse them, and what format they can absorb. But the dashboard becomes spiritually dangerous when it becomes authoritative—when it dictates what you will say, how you will say it, and who you will become in order to keep the numbers rising.

When that happens, three distortions typically follow:

1. **You begin to prefer content that "wins" over content that heals.** Outrage performs. Patience does not. Mockery travels faster than mercy.

2. **You begin to speak for the algorithm rather than for Christ.** You shape your tone and message to what the system rewards, not to what discipleship requires.

3. **You begin to interpret growth as divine approval and decline as failure.** This is subtle spiritual vanity: baptizing the platform's feedback as if it were God's voice.

Jesus does not promise the Church constant public success. He promises that those who abide will bear fruit, and that pruning—loss, limitation, and apparent setback—often belongs to fruitfulness: "Every branch of mine that bears fruit, he prunes, that it may bear more fruit" (John 15:2). Sometimes what looks like decline on the platform is pruning from the Lord: a mercy that rescues you from self-deception, purifies your motives, and re-centers your work on discipleship.

Abiding and bearing fruit: Christ's measure

Jesus' image is both comforting and severe. Comforting, because it tells you that the source of fruitfulness is not your cleverness, your charisma, or your consistency. It is communion with Christ: "Abide in me, and I in you. As the branch cannot bear fruit by itself... neither can you, unless you abide in me" (John 15:4). Severe, because it insists that ministry severed from Christ becomes spiritually barren—no matter how impressive the numbers.

Online work, especially, can tempt you into a life of constant output with minimal abiding. You post, respond, research, record, edit, and argue until the soul grows thin. Then you try to produce spiritual fruit from a branch that is drying out. Christ's warning is quiet but absolute: "Apart from me you can do nothing" (John 15:5). Not "you can do less," or "you can do a little." Nothing that truly counts as fruit in the Kingdom.

So the first question behind all evaluation is: **Does this work flow from abiding?** Do you pray? Do you repent? Do you worship? Do you listen? Do you submit your speech to Christ before you broadcast it to thousands? Or is your online ministry a substitute for communion with God?

Fruitfulness begins there.

God gives the growth: your labor is real, but it is not ultimate

The second corrective comes from Paul: "I planted, Apollos watered, but God gave the growth. So neither he who plants nor he who waters is anything, but only God who gives the growth" (1 Corinthians 3:6–7, RSV). This is a necessary medicine for online creators, because platforms train you to think of growth as the direct product of technique. If you optimize the thumbnail, sharpen the hook, target the right controversy, post at the right time, and ride the right trend, the numbers rise. In that environment, it is easy to import a business logic into evangelism: *If I do X correctly, I will get Y results.*

But the Gospel is not an algorithm.

Paul does not deny labor. He does not say planting and watering are meaningless. He says they are not ultimate. God alone gives growth. That means two things at once:

1. **You must work.** Faithfulness involves real preparation, skill, courage, discipline, and care. Planting and watering are your vocation.

2. **You must relinquish control.** You cannot force conversion, manufacture repentance, or guarantee spiritual fruit through technique. Growth belongs to God.

This frees the Christian creator from a form of desperation. You are not called to be omnipotent. You are called to be faithful. And faithfulness often looks unimpressive by the world's standards.

A single conversation that helps a person return to prayer may be more fruitful than a viral clip that inflames a thousand angry reactions. A patient explanation that clarifies the Gospel for a confused seeker may "perform" poorly but bear real fruit. Paul's framework allows you to pursue excellence without idolatry and to accept obscurity without despair.

What counts as fruit? The Gospel gives a concrete answer

Platforms define "fruit" as engagement. Scripture defines fruit as transformed life.

Paul names the fruit with astonishing clarity: "The fruit of the Spirit is love, joy, peace, patience, kindness, goodness, faithfulness, gentleness, self-control" (Galatians 5:22–23, RSV). This list is a spiritual measuring rod for online ministry—both for the audience and for the creator.

Here is an uncomfortable but necessary question: **Is your online presence producing these fruits in you?** If your content creation makes you consistently less patient, less gentle, more reactive, more suspicious, more addicted to conflict, more contemptuous, then the work is harming the worker—even if the audience is growing.

And another question: **Is your content encouraging these fruits in others?** If people come away more hateful, more anxious, more tribal, more cruel, more eager to denounce than to pray, then something is wrong—even if they call it "discernment" and even if they are doctrinally correct. Orthodoxy without charity is not mature discipleship; it is a brittle imitation of it.

Fruit is not only internal. It also includes concrete discipleship outcomes: prayer, repentance, worship, reconciliation, a desire for Scripture, renewed commitment to Christian community, increased compassion for neighbor, and perseverance in holiness. Not all of these outcomes can be measured, and many will remain hidden. That is part of the humility of ministry. But the inability to measure fruit does not excuse us from seeking it.

A fourfold measure: fidelity, clarity, charity, and discipleship outcomes

To evaluate online Christian work without being enslaved to metrics, it helps to adopt a set of criteria that are explicitly biblical and pastoral. The following fourfold measure can become a practical "examination of conscience" for creators.

1) Fidelity: is it true to Christ and his Gospel?

Fidelity asks: *Does this content faithfully represent Scripture, the Church's teaching (as you understand it within your tradition), and the heart of the Gospel?* Or is it distorted by partisan slogans, conspiratorial thinking, or selective quoting designed to produce outrage?

Fidelity includes intellectual honesty: acknowledging what you do not know, correcting errors publicly when needed, and refusing to repeat claims you cannot verify. If God is the author of truth, truthfulness is not optional.

2) Clarity: can a real person understand it?

Clarity asks: *Is this content actually understandable to the audience God has given you?* Online platforms can reward insider language and coded tribal signals. But evangelism and catechesis require clear speech. Many people listening are seekers, new believers, or wounded former Christians. If your content assumes too much, they will misunderstand—and misunderstanding can become scandal.

Clarity also includes structural clarity: defining terms, distinguishing opinion from doctrine, and separating what is certain from what is speculative.

3) Charity: does it reflect the mind of Christ toward persons?

Charity asks: *Is this content shaped by love of neighbor, even when it rebukes?* Does it treat opponents as human beings made in the image of God, or as objects for ridicule? Does it invite the sinner to repentance, or merely entertain the righteous with denunciation?

Charity is not weakness. It is obedience. And it is evangelistically strategic in the best sense: many unbelievers have been inoculated against Christianity because they have only seen Christian contempt. Charity re-opens the possibility that the Gospel is actually good news.

4) Discipleship outcomes: does it move people toward abiding?

This is the hardest to "count," but it is the most important. Discipleship outcomes ask: *Does this content move people toward prayer, Scripture, repentance, obedience, worship, and life in Christian community?* Or does it keep them circling in spectatorship—watching religious arguments as entertainment?

Here is a practical test: if someone watched your content for six months, would they be more likely to pray, read Scripture, love neighbor, forgive enemies, and join themselves to a community of faith? Or would they simply be better at online debates?

Virality is not always a blessing (and obscurity is not always a failure)

Online virality can happen for many reasons that have nothing to do with fruit: novelty, controversy, outrage, humor, timing, controversy between factions, or the algorithm's unpredictable preference. Sometimes viral reach can be used for good, and Christians should not be ashamed of being heard. But viral reach is spiritually ambiguous. It can expand temptation faster than it expands holiness.

Likewise, obscurity is not necessarily failure. Some ministries are hidden by design: quiet catechesis, careful pastoral work, small communities, patient Bible teaching, and steady witness to a niche audience that truly needs it. Jesus' imagery of abiding and fruit implies that the deepest realities are often not immediately visible.

Paul's reminder—"God gave the growth" (1 Corinthians 3:6)—can protect you from interpreting your analytics as a spiritual verdict.

Practical practices for creators

A discipleship practice: adopt a "fruit audit"

Once a month, review your work using Galatians 5:22–23. Ask:

- Has my online ministry increased love, joy, peace, patience, kindness, goodness, faithfulness, gentleness, self-control in me?
- Has it tended to produce these fruits in my audience—at least among those most committed?
- Where has my work produced the opposite (anger, contempt, anxiety, impatience, harshness)?

Write down one concrete change you will make for the next month. Not a change to optimize numbers—a change to cultivate fruit.

A fidelity practice: separate "witness" from "hot take"

Before posting about a controversial event, ask:

1. Do I know the facts?
2. Can I cite reliable sources?
3. Is this necessary for discipleship?
4. Have I prayed first?

If the answer is no, consider silence as an act of obedience.

A clarity practice: include next steps that lead to abiding

At the end of teaching content, regularly give one simple next step that points to Christ rather than to your channel: a brief prayer, a short Scripture passage to read, an act of reconciliation, a suggestion to seek a local church or pastor, a work of mercy.

This is one way to "teach them to observe" rather than merely to react.

Reflection questions

1. When your numbers rise, what happens in your heart: gratitude and humility—or hunger and anxiety? What does that reveal?

2. When your numbers fall, do you become tempted to intensify controversy, sharpen ridicule, or compromise fidelity?

3. Which of the four measures do you neglect most: fidelity, clarity, charity, or discipleship outcomes?

4. If God asked you to be faithful in obscurity for years, could you accept that as a genuine vocation?

5. What "fruit of the Spirit" is most threatened by your online activity right now?

Closing prayer

Lord Jesus Christ, true Vine and source of all life, keep me abiding in you. Free me from the hunger for applause and the fear of decline. Purify my work so that it bears the fruit of your Spirit—love, joy, peace, patience, kindness, goodness, faithfulness, gentleness, and self-control. Make me a faithful servant who plants and waters with care, trusting you alone to give the growth. Amen.

Chapter 3

A Rule of Life for Digital Mission

Online ministry can be a genuine act of love. It can also become a slow spiritual unraveling. The danger is not only what you might encounter online; it is what constant output can do to the inner life of the person producing it. A creator can begin with zeal and end with exhaustion. A teacher can begin with sincerity and end with irritability. A witness can begin with humility and end with vanity. The platform does not ask whether your soul is being saved. It asks whether you are posting.

This is why anyone engaged in Christian digital mission needs a rule of life. A rule is not a rigid schedule meant to earn God's favor. It is a pattern that protects what is living. It is a trellis for the vine. Without a rule, you will be governed by the platform's rhythms: urgency, reaction, endless comparison, and the subtle belief that you are only faithful if you are always visible.

Scripture gives us the pattern. Jesus orders mission around prayer. Mark tells us that even amid demands and crowds, "in the morning, a great while before day, he rose and went out to a lonely place, and there he prayed" (Mark 1:35, RSV). That rhythm is deeply instructive. Jesus does not treat prayer as what happens after ministry when energy remains. He treats prayer as what makes ministry obedient. If the Son prays before the Father while carrying the burden of proclamation, then any Christian who speaks publicly must place prayer at the center as well. Otherwise the work becomes mere output, and the soul becomes dry.

Acts offers the communal shape of the Christian life: "And they devoted themselves to the apostles' teaching and fellowship, to the breaking of bread and the prayers" (Acts 2:42, RSV). Notice the balance. The early Church is not only "teaching." It is also fellowship. It is worship and sacramental life. It is prayer. Digital work can support these realities, but it cannot replace them. Online mission that is disconnected from embodied Christian community eventually becomes distorted, because it loses the ordinary protections God provides: being known, being corrected, serving real neighbors, worshiping with real people, and learning love in the slow school of relationships.

Finally, Paul's command presses the whole life toward God: "Pray constantly" (1 Thessalonians 5:17, RSV). This is not a demand for nonstop words, but for a heart oriented to God, regularly returning to him. For the digital missionary, it is also a practical antidote to the platform's formation. Prayer slows the pace. Prayer reveals motives. Prayer purifies tone. Prayer helps you speak less from adrenaline and more from peace.

A rule of life for digital mission therefore needs to include at least seven elements: prayer, study, accountability, rest, confession and repentance, local church/community, and deliberate limits. These are not separate compartments; they interlock. Prayer without study can become vague. Study without prayer can become pride. Accountability without rest can become burnout. Limits without repentance can become mere strategy. The point is a coherent rhythm that keeps your online witness connected to the ordinary Christian life.

Begin with prayer, because everything else depends on it. If you speak about God more than you speak to God, you will eventually lose the spiritual realism that makes witness credible. A simple, faithful pattern is to pray before the day's noise begins, to pause briefly before posting, and to surrender outcomes afterward. That surrender is important. Without it, you will live chained to the refresh button, reading your analytics as if they were God's verdict.

Add study, because Christians who teach must love truth. Online environments reward the appearance of knowledge, and they punish hesitation. A rule of life insists that you will not pretend. It makes space for real Scripture reading and serious formation, so that you do not become a dispenser of confident half-truths. Study also supports humility, because genuine learning reveals how much there is you do not know. It trains you to speak carefully, to verify claims, and to correct yourself when needed.

Add accountability, because Christianity is not a solo vocation. Online platforms tempt creators into a kind of independence that feels like freedom but often becomes a spiritual trap. A rule of life insists that you are under authority and within community. That may mean a pastor, a spiritual director, trusted peers, or a mature friend who has permission to tell you the truth. Without such relationships, you are likely to confuse criticism with persecution and applause with anointing. Accountability protects you from your own blind spots and from the slow inflation of ego that public speech often produces.

Add rest, because the Gospel does not require you to be constantly available. The platform will gladly consume your life. It will train you to believe that silence is failure and that absence is disobedience. But God builds rest into human life as a sign that we are not gods. A digital Sabbath—whether a full day or a consistent block of time—becomes an act of faith. It declares that Christ is Lord, not the algorithm, and that the world will not collapse if you stop posting.

Add confession and repentance, because public ministry without repentance becomes hypocrisy. A creator who speaks about sin and grace must live under the same mercy and discipline. This means examining the conscience, acknowledging when you spoke harshly, correcting errors without defensiveness, and repairing harm when you misrepresent others. The platform trains people to double down; the Gospel trains people to turn around. Public repentance, when needed, can be one of the most powerful forms of discipleship you can model.

Add local church and community, because disciples are formed in embodied life. Online ministry must never subtly replace worship, fellowship, and service. The early Church "devoted themselves" to these practices (Acts 2:42). A Christian creator must likewise be anchored in a community where they are not merely a voice but a member—known, corrected, needed, and loved. This prevents the dangerous illusion that Christian life is mainly content and commentary.

Finally, add limits, because boundaries are love. The internet blurs privacy, encourages oversharing, and can invite "confession-like" DMs that place both creator and vulnerable person in a spiritually unsafe situation. A rule of life includes limits on what you will share, how you will respond, and when you will disengage. It includes a commitment not to post in anger, not to amplify rumors, and not to let parasocial dependence grow. These limits are not a lack of compassion; they are the protection of souls.

The purpose of a rule of life is not to make you impressive. It is to make you faithful. It is to keep your digital mission rooted in the pattern of Jesus and the life of the Church. When your online ministry is sustained by prayer, formed by study, protected by accountability, refreshed by rest, purified by repentance, anchored in community, and guarded by wise limits, you are far more likely to speak with truth and charity. You are more likely to produce disciples rather than spectators. And you are less likely to lose your soul while trying to help others.

If you must choose one principle to hold above the rest, let it be this: the platform is a tool, but Christ is Lord. Your rule of life exists to keep that order intact.

Reflection questions

1. What currently governs your online work: prayer and discernment—or urgency and reaction?
2. Which part of Acts 2:42 is weakest in your life right now: teaching, fellowship, breaking of bread, or prayers?
3. What limit do you most resist—and why?
4. Are you becoming more patient and gentler through this work, or more reactive and harsher?
5. Who has real permission to correct you?

Closing prayer

Lord Jesus Christ, who rose early to pray, teach me your rhythm. Root my digital mission in prayer, in the teaching of your word, in fellowship, and in the life of your Church. Give me humility to receive correction, courage to set limits, and wisdom to rest. May my words be true, charitable, and ordered to discipleship, so that you may be known and loved. Amen.

Chapter 4

Begin With Self-Conversion: The Beam and the Speck

One of the strangest temptations in online Christian speech is how easily it can make us feel holy while leaving us unchanged. The internet offers a kind of righteousness-by-commentary: we denounce the sins of the age, expose the errors of others, and take our place among the "clear-eyed" and the "faithful." We may even quote Scripture while doing it. And yet, at the end of the day, we may not have prayed, repented, forgiven anyone, or performed a single work of mercy. We have "spoken for truth," but we have not been converted.

This is why the beginning of Christian online mission must be self-conversion. Not because we must be perfect before we speak, but because we must never forget what we are: sinners saved by grace, servants of a holy God, disciples still being formed. When Christian speech begins with the sins of everyone else, it quietly trains both the speaker and the audience to avoid the Gospel's first demand: repent.

Jesus addresses this danger directly in the Sermon on the Mount: "Judge not, that you be not judged. For with the judgment you pronounce you will be judged... Why do you see the speck that is in your brother's eye, but do not notice the beam that is in your own eye? ... You hypocrite, first take the beam out of your own eye, and then you will see clearly to take the speck out of your brother's eye" (Matthew 7:1–5, RSV).

This passage is often misunderstood. Jesus is not abolishing moral discernment. He is not saying that sin is imaginary or that truth does not matter. He is confronting a particular spiritual posture: the posture of hypocrisy, condemnation, and blindness—where we hold others to strict standards while granting ourselves a wide, comfortable mercy. His command is not "pretend there are no specks." His command is "first take the beam out of your own eye." He teaches an order of operations. Repentance comes first, and only then does the believer gain the clear sight needed to offer correction as medicine rather than as a weapon.

Online platforms make this teaching urgent. They reward denunciation because denunciation is fast, emotionally satisfying, and instantly legible. It signals group belonging. It also creates an addictive loop: the creator feels righteous, the audience feels affirmed, the algorithm rewards the heat, and the cycle intensifies. When this becomes habitual, outrage quietly replaces repentance. Denouncing others becomes a substitute for examining oneself. This is why public denunciation without inner conversion corrodes Christian witness: it trains the soul away from humility, and it trains the audience away from mercy.

Jesus warns that judgment is never neutral: "With the judgment you pronounce you will be judged, and the measure you give will be the measure you get" (Matthew 7:2). In online life, this becomes almost literal. If you build your presence on harshness, you will receive harshness. If you build your identity on flawless correctness, you will be punished whenever you misspeak. Yet the deeper danger is not the reaction you receive; it is the spiritual deformation you suffer. A person who repeatedly speaks in condemnation can gradually lose the capacity for compassion. A person who rarely repents can gradually lose the capacity for joy. The Gospel begins to feel like a weapon rather than a healing word.

Self-conversion begins when we stop treating ourselves as the exception. The "beam" Jesus names is not necessarily a scandalous sin that would shock your audience. Often the beam is more subtle and therefore more dangerous, because it can hide behind religious language. Pride can disguise itself as zeal. Vanity can disguise itself as mission. Harshness can disguise itself as courage. Envy can disguise itself as discernment. Fear can disguise itself as doctrinal militancy. These interior sins distort spiritual sight. They make us interpret people as threats rather than neighbors, and they make us believe that winning is the same as witnessing.

At this point, many Christian creators feel trapped between two bad options: either remain silent about sin and error, or speak with severity and be applauded for it. Jesus offers a third way. He does not say, "Never address the speck." He says, "First take the beam out of your own eye, and then you will see clearly to take the speck out of your brother's eye" (Matthew 7:5). That "then" matters. Jesus wants correction to be possible, but he wants it to come from humility and clarity, not from hypocrisy and contempt. A Christian who has learned repentance can correct without needing to humiliate. A Christian who knows his own fragility can speak firmly without becoming cruel. A Christian who remembers mercy can call for repentance without acting as though he stands above judgment.

This is where Psalm 139 becomes a necessary prayer for anyone speaking publicly in the name of Christ: "Search me, O God, and know my heart! Try me and know my thoughts! And see if there be any wicked way in me, and lead me in the way everlasting!" (Psalm 139:23–24, RSV). The psalmist does not merely ask God to forgive him; he asks God to examine him. He acknowledges that self-knowledge is limited, that the heart can deceive itself, and that we need divine light to see ourselves truthfully. In the digital world—where affirmation is immediate and communities can reinforce blind spots—this prayer is not simply devotional. It is protection.

Public denunciation without visible repentance also damages Christian witness because it contradicts the Gospel's own pattern. The Gospel begins with the confession that "all have sinned" and that salvation is mercy before achievement. When Christian speech is dominated by condemnation, outsiders do not hear good news; they hear a courtroom. Many have never met a Christian who speaks strongly while loving gently. Many have never seen a Christian correct himself publicly. Many have never seen a Christian disagree with another believer without contempt. Yet when they do encounter these things, it can re-open the possibility that Christianity is not merely tribal conflict with religious language, but an encounter with holiness and mercy.

Self-conversion cannot remain an idea. It must become a practice, otherwise the beam stays in place while we keep talking about specks. A simple discipline is to pause before posting and ask what is driving you. Are you seeking to help someone toward repentance and hope, or are you venting? Are you aiming at clarity, or at applause? Would you still post this if it brought you no engagement? Have you prayed first, even briefly, asking God to purify your motive and guard your tongue? These questions do not make you timid; they make you honest.

It is also wise to adopt a regular examination of conscience shaped by your public speech. At least weekly, ask whether you exaggerated for effect, assumed motives without evidence, enjoyed humiliation, or trained your audience toward anger rather than holiness. When you find sin—and you will—do not excuse it with "that's just how the internet works." Repent. If you misrepresented a person, correct it. If you passed along something unverified, retract it. If you spoke harshly, acknowledge it and seek to repair harm. This is not weakness. It is integrity. It is discipleship practiced in public.

Sometimes the most evangelically powerful act a Christian creator can do is model repentance plainly. The platform trains people to double down. The Gospel trains people to turn around. When you turn around publicly, you show that Christianity is not a performance of perfection but a life of continual conversion.

Finally, remember that correction is meant for healing. Jesus' warning about judgment does not forbid naming sin; it forbids contempt. The Christian can denounce sin and error while still speaking as a physician of souls rather than as an executioner. If you want your correction to bear fruit, your audience must sense that you genuinely desire the good of the person you critique—and that you would rather see them repent than be destroyed. In a world addicted to humiliation, that desire becomes a sign of Christ.

The beam and the speck are therefore not merely a rule for online etiquette; they are a summary of the Christian life. The disciple is always being purified, always being corrected, always being led more deeply into truth. Christian online influencing that does not begin here will eventually become harsh, performative, and brittle. But Christian online influencing that begins with self-conversion can become something rare: firm without cruelty, truthful without pride, courageous without contempt, and persuasive because it sounds like mercy.

"Search me, O God, and know my heart... and lead me in the way everlasting" (Psalm 139:23–24). That is the prayer that removes the beam. And only then, with clear sight, can we help others with the specks that truly harm them.

Discussion Questions

1. When you correct others online, what is most active in your heart: love for their good, fear for "your side," or a desire to be seen as right?

2. What "beam" is most likely to distort your vision in online ministry—pride, vanity, harshness, envy, fear, or something subtler?

3. How often do you model repentance publicly when you speak wrongly or treat someone unfairly? What keeps you from doing so?

4. Does your online presence make you more patient and gentler over time, or more reactive and suspicious? What patterns suggest the answer?

5. If someone watched your content for six months, would they learn how to repent, forgive, and pray—or mainly how to denounce?

Closing Prayer

Search me, O God, and know my heart. Try me and know my thoughts. Reveal the sins I excuse and the pride I hide. Remove the beam from my eye, that I may see clearly and speak truth without contempt. Give me humility to repent, courage to repair harm, and love that seeks the salvation of my neighbor. Lead me in the way everlasting, through Jesus Christ our Lord. Amen.

Chapter 5

Weakness, Reluctance, and Calling: Power Made Perfect

The online world loves the image of strength. It rewards confidence, quick certainty, and the appearance of unshakable control. It prefers the creator who speaks as though nothing troubles him, as though every question has already been settled, as though every opponent is easily dismissed. Even in Christian spaces, the persona that often performs best is the persona of mastery: the fearless truth-teller, the spiritual warrior, the one who always has the perfect answer in the perfect tone.

But Scripture tells a different story about how God works.

Again and again, God calls the reluctant. He chooses the weak. He sends the stammerer. He entrusts holy work to fragile people who cannot plausibly take credit for the results. This is not an accident. It is one of God's primary methods of revealing that salvation is not the achievement of the strong but the gift of grace. When Christians forget this pattern, online ministry can drift into a kind of savior-complex—subtle or obvious—where the creator begins to present himself as the one who must fix the Church, rescue the confused, and defeat the enemies. That posture may feel heroic. It may also be deeply unchristian.

The Gospel does not need our performance of strength. It needs our faithful obedience, offered in humility, so that God's power—not ours—can be seen.

God's answer to weakness

Paul gives us one of the most important lines for public ministry. After describing a deep personal affliction, he reports the Lord's response: "My grace is sufficient for you, for my power is made perfect in weakness" (2 Corinthians 12:9, RSV). Paul's reaction is not resignation but a radical reorientation of how ministry works: "I will all the more gladly boast of my weaknesses, that the power of Christ may rest upon me... for when I am weak, then I am strong" (2 Corinthians 12:9–10).

This is not sentimental. Paul is not romanticizing pain. He is confessing a spiritual reality: God's power is often clearest where human self-reliance has been stripped away. Weakness, when joined to faith, becomes a stage on which grace can be seen. And weakness also protects ministry from a subtle idolatry: the idolatry of thinking that the mission depends on our personality, our rhetorical skill, our energy, or our ability to dominate the conversation.

Online platforms encourage the opposite. They pressure you to appear invulnerable, constantly capable, always certain, always "on." They reward the creator who never hesitates and never admits limitations. Yet Paul's theology says that the Christian leader who refuses weakness is refusing one of God's primary instruments for revealing grace.

God chooses what the world does not

Paul presses this even further when he describes God's pattern of choosing: "God chose what is foolish in the world to shame the wise, God chose what is weak in the world to shame the strong...

so that no human being might boast in the presence of God" (1 Corinthians 1:27–29, RSV). In other words, God intentionally selects unlikely instruments so that the glory cannot plausibly be assigned to the instrument.

This is not a rejection of intelligence, competence, or excellence. Scripture honors wisdom. The point is that God refuses to let the Church become a monument to human greatness. He wants the world to see that the Gospel is not a technique the clever have mastered, but a salvation God has accomplished.

That matters enormously online, because the internet makes it easy to boast. It makes it easy to measure yourself against others, to build a following, to cultivate a persona, and to interpret success as personal superiority. It also makes it easy to despise "ordinary" Christians—people who do not speak well, do not know the newest arguments, do not have a platform, do not have influence. Yet God repeatedly does his deepest work through the ordinary, the overlooked, and the imperfect. If you are called to digital mission, you must guard yourself against the assumption that "important Christians" are the visible ones.

Moses and the reluctant call

The pattern is already clear in the Old Testament. When God calls Moses, Moses does not respond with confident heroism. He responds with reluctance and honest limitation: "Oh, my Lord, I am not eloquent... but I am slow of speech and of tongue" (Exodus 4:10, RSV). Moses is not posturing. He is naming what he perceives as a real incapacity for the task.

God does not deny Moses' limitation as though it were imaginary. Instead he locates Moses' calling inside God's own sovereignty: "Who has made man's mouth?... Is it not I, the LORD? Now therefore go, and I will be with your mouth and teach you what you shall speak" (Exodus 4:11–12, RSV). Moses is sent not because he is naturally equipped, but because God will be with him.

That is the heart of calling. Calling is not first a matter of your personality being perfectly suited to the task. It is first a matter of God's presence and God's purpose. The Lord's promise—"I will be with your mouth"—is a reminder that ministry is not ultimately self-expression. It is obedience supported by grace.

This is especially important for online ministry because platforms tempt us to treat speaking as self-display. Our "voice" becomes our brand. Our uniqueness becomes our selling point. We can begin to speak more to maintain an image than to obey a calling. Moses is a corrective: he is not building a brand. He is obeying a summons, and he is doing so while aware of his own limits.

Resisting the savior-complex

A savior-complex in digital ministry does not usually begin with conscious arrogance. It often begins with genuine concern. You see confusion, scandal, suffering, and deception, and you want to help. That is good. But gradually, if you are not careful, the sense of responsibility can inflate. You begin to feel as though everything depends on you. You begin to interpret criticism as persecution, because you have cast yourself as the hero of the story. You begin to speak as though you are the last faithful voice, or the only one willing to tell the truth.

This posture is spiritually dangerous for at least two reasons. First, it is not true. Christ is Lord of his Church. The Spirit is at work in places you cannot see. God's kingdom is not fragile in the way your ego suggests. Second, it is spiritually corrosive. It produces anxiety, harshness, and contempt, because a person who believes he must save everyone will eventually treat people as obstacles when they resist. The savior-complex always turns others into either trophies or enemies.

Paul's confession—"when I am weak, then I am strong"—cuts against this. It reminds you that you are not the Savior. You are not the Messiah. You are not even the main character. You are an earthen vessel. The treasure is Christ.

Online Christian work becomes healthier when it is marked by a different spirit: a willingness to say, "I cannot carry the world, but I can be faithful today." A willingness to admit, "I do not know," rather than improvising certainty. A willingness to step back, rest, and pray, because the Church is not held together by your content calendar.

The gift of limitation

One of the most countercultural virtues for a Christian creator is accepting limitation without shame. Limitation can take many forms: lack of time, lack of skill, mental or physical health constraints, family responsibilities, a small audience, a restricted platform, seasons of silence. The platform teaches you to interpret limitations as failure. Scripture teaches you to interpret them as opportunities for humility and dependence.

God often keeps his servants small so that they do not become intoxicated with their own influence. God sometimes withholds the kind of success that would destroy a person's soul. And God often uses hidden faithfulness to do work that visible "success" could never do.

This does not mean you refuse growth out of false piety. It means you refuse to measure your vocation by scale. If God gives you reach, receive it with trembling and gratitude. If God gives you obscurity, receive it with peace and fidelity. Either way, the call is the same: "Now therefore go, and I will be with your mouth" (Exodus 4:12).

A different posture for digital mission

If you want to resist the savior-complex and embrace God's pattern of power made perfect in weakness, your posture online will change. You will begin to sound less like a performer and more like a witness. You will speak with more patience because you no longer need to dominate. You will correct with more mercy because you remember your own fragility. You will stop treating every controversy as a battlefield you must enter, and you will start discerning whether engaging will actually serve discipleship.

You will also become freer to be human. You will be able to say, without shame, that you are tired, that you need prayer, that you need rest, that you need correction. You will become more able to give glory to God rather than to your own courage or cleverness. And you will find, paradoxically, that this humility often increases credibility. People are starving for honesty, especially spiritual honesty. A Christian who speaks as a forgiven sinner rather than as a flawless judge often becomes more persuasive, not less.

The world admires strength. The Gospel reveals a crucified Lord. The world rewards mastery. God chooses what is weak. The platform trains you to appear invulnerable. Christ trains you to depend on grace. If you accept this pattern, your digital mission will become less exhausting and more faithful, because you will no longer be trying to be the Savior. You will be pointing to him.

Discussion Questions

1. When you feel "called" to speak online, do you feel peace and clarity, or do you feel frantic pressure as though everything depends on you? What does that reveal?

2. In what ways are you tempted to project invulnerability online? What would humble honesty look like without oversharing?

3. Do you interpret your limitations—time, energy, skill, reach—as failures to hide, or as realities to offer to God?

4. Where might a savior-complex be creeping into your online work (needing to fix everyone, fighting every battle, craving to be the decisive voice)?

5. How might your content change if you truly believed, "My grace is sufficient for you" (2 Corinthians 12:9)?

Closing Prayer

Lord Jesus Christ, you have shown your power through the weakness of the cross and the mercy of grace. Deliver me from pride, from the hunger to appear strong, and from the illusion that I must save your Church. Teach me to accept my limitations without shame and to offer them to you in obedience. When I am weak, let your strength be revealed. When I am reluctant, be with my mouth and teach me what I shall speak. Keep me humble, faithful, and free, so that the treasure of the Gospel may be seen in an earthen vessel, and all glory may be yours. Amen.

Chapter 6

"He Must Increase, I Must Decrease": Escaping the Cult of Personality

Christian online ministry lives in a dangerous neighborhood: the attention economy. Platforms are designed to elevate personalities. They reward the recognizable voice, the magnetic persona, the creator who becomes a "must-watch" identity. Over time, this can quietly reshape the meaning of ministry. The work can shift from proclaiming Christ to performing a self. The audience can shift from being seekers and disciples to being fans. And the creator can shift from being a servant to being the center.

This is not a problem confined to celebrities. It can happen on any scale. A small account can become a tiny kingdom; a large platform can become an empire. The underlying temptation is the same: to take the spiritual energy that belongs to God and redirect it—subtly or openly—toward the self.

Scripture gives us a model for refusing that temptation in one of the most arresting one-sentence statements of Christian humility: "He must increase, but I must decrease" (John 3:30, RSV). John the Baptist speaks these words at the exact moment when many modern creators would panic: when the crowds begin to shift away from him and toward Jesus. His disciples come to him with what sounds like an alarming report: the one John baptized is now becoming the next star, and "all are going to him" (cf. John 3:26). In the logic of the platform, that is a threat. It is loss—loss of attention, loss of relevance, loss of influence.

John does not respond with rivalry. He responds with joy. He understands his vocation. He is not the Bridegroom; he is the friend of the Bridegroom. He is not the center; he is the signpost. His entire identity is structured around pointing away from himself. He does not cling to visibility as though it were his rightful reward. He receives decreasing as obedience. He embraces being surpassed because his purpose was never to be the destination.

This is the first spiritual test of Christian online influence: can you rejoice when Christ is served, even if you are not the one being noticed?

The platform temptation in this chapter: being "the point" while talking about Jesus

Platforms reward personality, and personality is not inherently evil. God uses human voice, style, humor, warmth, and particularity. People relate to persons. The problem is not having a personality. The problem is allowing the personality to become the product and Christ to become the branding.

A Christian creator may begin by proclaiming Jesus and end by building a world in which Jesus is a supporting character. The channel becomes the "place" where people belong. The creator becomes the arbiter of truth. The audience learns to measure Christianity by loyalty to that voice, that style, that camp, that "team." This is how cults of personality form—not always through explicit claims, but through subtle habits: the creator is always right, always justified, always the one who sees clearly; critics are always malicious; disagreements are betrayal; and discipleship becomes indistinguishable from allegiance.

This is spiritual danger not only for the audience, but for the creator. The cult of personality flatters the ego, and flattery is one of the fastest ways to lose contact with reality. It also makes repentance harder. A person who must maintain an image will resist correction. A person who must remain the hero will interpret humility as weakness. A person who needs admiration will begin to preach what pleases rather than what saves.

John the Baptist's sentence—"I must decrease"—is therefore not a poetic motto. It is a spiritual safeguard.

"What we preach is not ourselves"

Paul states the same principle with apostolic bluntness: "For what we preach is not ourselves, but Jesus Christ as Lord, with ourselves as your servants for Jesus' sake" (2 Corinthians 4:5, RSV). This is a defining line for Christian communication. It draws a clear boundary between proclamation and self-promotion.

Paul does not say, "We preach ourselves and also Jesus." He says the opposite. Jesus is Lord; we are servants. The point of Christian speech is not to magnify the speaker. It is to magnify Christ. Even when the message is delivered through a particular human personality, the personality must remain transparent—like a window, not a mirror. A window lets light through. A mirror reflects the self.

Online platforms are engineered to turn every window into a mirror. They encourage creators to become brands. They train audiences to form parasocial bonds, to attach emotionally to the persona, to feel defended by their "leader," and to feel personally threatened when that leader is criticized. All of this can happen while the creator sincerely believes he is "just doing ministry." That is why a Christian must examine not only what he says, but what his presence is forming in his audience.

John's joy is the antidote

John's humility is not grim self-hatred. It is joyful clarity. He knows his place in God's story, and that knowledge frees him from rivalry. He can decrease without becoming bitter because decreasing is not humiliation for him; it is fulfillment. His joy is not in his own prominence, but in Christ's coming.

This joy is a profound rebuke to the creator who cannot tolerate being surpassed, ignored, or forgotten. If your identity depends on being necessary, you will eventually become controlling. If your identity depends on being admired, you will eventually become manipulative. But if your identity is anchored in Christ, you can serve freely. You can rejoice when others succeed. You can share attention rather than hoard it. You can step back when stepping back serves the Gospel. You can even become "less," because your worth is not measured by visibility.

John also shows us that it is possible to be a powerful public voice without becoming self-absorbed. He is courageous. He is clear. He is uncompromising. And yet he refuses self-worship. He refuses to make himself the point. He speaks as a witness, not as a celebrity.

How to recognize a cult of personality forming

A cult of personality is not always obvious at first. It often appears as "strong community" and "clear teaching." But there are warning signs that should sober any Christian creator.

One sign is when the community's emotional energy is primarily directed toward the creator rather than toward Christ. Another is when criticism of the creator is treated as an attack on the faith itself. Another is when followers begin to imitate the creator's tone more than they imitate Christ's character—especially if the tone is harsh, mocking, or perpetually outraged. Another is when the creator becomes unable to say, "I was wrong," because the persona must remain invulnerable. Another is when the creator begins to speak as though he alone is the trustworthy guide and everyone else is compromised.

The remedy is not paranoia. The remedy is intentional humility and a deliberate re-centering on Christ.

Practices that help Christ increase

A creator who wants Christ to increase must cultivate habits that pull attention away from the self and toward the Lord. One of the simplest is to regularly direct people toward Scripture, prayer, worship, and local community rather than toward the next piece of content. When your content ends with "follow me for more," it can easily become self-referential. When it ends with "pray this," "read this passage," "seek reconciliation," "speak with your pastor," "serve your neighbor," it becomes discipleship-shaped.

Another practice is to honor other voices. When you share good work by others, you weaken the illusion that your audience needs only you. You also model generosity rather than rivalry. A third practice is to build structures of accountability so that your influence is not unchecked. If you are under correction, your audience learns that you are not the final authority. A fourth practice is to accept seasons of silence and decrease without panic. If you cannot step away, you are not free. If you cannot lose engagement without despair, you have likely attached your identity to visibility.

Most importantly, a creator must learn to pray John's sentence sincerely: "He must increase, but I must decrease" (John 3:30). That prayer will sometimes be answered by growth that humbles you and forces you to rely on grace. It will sometimes be answered by limitation that purifies you and saves you from vanity. Either way, it is mercy.

The freedom of being a servant

Paul's phrase "your servants for Jesus' sake" (2 Corinthians 4:5) is not a demotion. It is liberation. If you are a servant, you do not need to be worshiped. You do not need to be invulnerable. You do not need to win every argument. You do not need to maintain a perfect image. You can be corrected. You can be overlooked. You can tell the truth without needing to be applauded for it. You can speak firmly without becoming cruel, because you are not defending an ego. You are serving a Lord.

This is what platforms cannot understand. Platforms build empires of self. The Gospel builds a kingdom where the King is Christ and the servants are free.

John the Baptist points the way: decrease without resentment, rejoice when Christ is magnified, and measure success by faithfulness to your calling rather than by the size of your crowd. The Christian creator is at his best when people leave his content thinking less about him and more about Jesus—when the spotlight has shifted, the heart has been stirred toward repentance and prayer, and Christ has increased.

Discussion Questions

1. If your audience began to shrink because Christ was being served more clearly somewhere else, could you rejoice the way John did? Why or why not?

2. In what subtle ways might your online work be training people to attach to you rather than to Christ?

3. How do you respond internally to criticism—do you consider it carefully, or do you immediately feel the need to defend your persona?

4. Are you building structures that direct people toward Scripture, prayer, and local community, or are you building habits that keep people revolving around your content?

5. What would "decreasing" look like in your current season—less posting, less arguing, more silence, more prayer, more sharing of other voices, or something else?

Closing Prayer

Lord Jesus Christ, you are the Lord of the Church and the only Savior of the world. Deliver me from the hunger to be noticed, from the temptation to build a kingdom around myself, and from the subtle worship of personality. Teach me the joy of John the Baptist: "He must increase, but I must decrease." Make my words transparent to your light, so that what I preach is not myself but you, Jesus Christ as Lord. Keep me humble, accountable, and free, that I may serve others for your sake and point every heart beyond me to you. Amen.

Chapter 7

Know the Truth—Because God Is the Author of Truth

Online life is full of certainty and short on wisdom. Platforms reward the confident voice, the quick conclusion, the sharp take, and the emotionally satisfying narrative. In that environment, "truth" can become a costume: a set of slogans, screenshots, and selectively framed quotations deployed to win a moment. Even Christian content can slip into this pattern. We may speak constantly about truth while practicing habits that make truth harder to find: repeating claims we have not verified, quoting out of context, caricaturing opponents, or treating our own tradition as though it were identical with God himself.

But Scripture does not allow Christians to treat truth casually. Truth is not a tool for victory; it is a reality to be loved, sought, and obeyed. And truth is not merely something "out there" in the world; it is grounded in God. If God is the Creator, then all that is true participates in his faithfulness. To love truth is therefore a spiritual act. It is part of worship. It is one way we honor the God who cannot lie.

Jesus makes the connection between truth and discipleship explicit: "If you continue in my word, you are truly my disciples, and you will know the truth, and the truth will make you free" (John 8:31–32, RSV). Notice how the sentence is structured. Truth is not separated from discipleship; it is the fruit of continuing in Christ's word. And the result of truth is not merely that we win arguments; the result is freedom. Freedom from deception, freedom from slavery to sin, freedom from fear, freedom from the need to maintain illusions.

That means the Christian online witness must resist two equal and opposite dangers. The first is arrogance: speaking as though we possess truth completely and purely, as though our understanding is flawless, as though correction is an insult. The second is relativism: treating truth as a matter of preference and reducing Christianity to "my perspective." The Gospel refuses both. It calls us to confidence in what God has revealed, and to humility about our own limitations.

The platform temptation in this chapter: certainty without formation

The internet makes it possible to sound informed without being formed. A person can collect arguments, memorize talking points, and quote authorities without learning the patient disciplines that actually produce competence: careful reading, historical awareness, the ability to distinguish levels of certainty, and the willingness to admit gaps in knowledge. Platforms often reward the appearance of mastery more than mastery itself.

This is especially dangerous in religious content, because religious claims shape lives. When Christians speak carelessly, we do not merely risk embarrassment; we risk scandal. We can confuse the seeker, harden the skeptic, burden the scrupulous, and mislead the vulnerable. We may also harm our own souls, because speaking falsely, even unintentionally, trains the heart away from reverence.

To know the truth, therefore, is not simply to "have opinions." It is to cultivate a love of what is real, a willingness to be corrected by reality, and a disciplined approach to learning that treats God's gifts with seriousness.

Truth as a Christian virtue

Paul gives a surprisingly practical guide for the Christian mind: "Whatever is true, whatever is honorable, whatever is just, whatever is pure, whatever is lovely, whatever is gracious… think about these things" (Philippians 4:8, RSV). He does not begin with controversy. He begins with the objects worthy of contemplation—truth, honor, justice, purity, loveliness, grace. This is not a call to naïve positivity. It is a call to intellectual and moral discipline: to train the mind to dwell on what is worthy, rather than being dragged around by whatever is loudest.

Online environments often train the opposite habit. They train us to dwell on what is outrageous, what is humiliating, what is suspicious, what is cynical. They make it feel "responsible" to be perpetually angry and perpetually alarmed. Yet Christian maturity requires a different mental posture. It requires attentiveness to truth, and also to what is honorable and just.

If God is the author of truth, then truthfulness is not merely an academic concern; it is a moral concern. Christians must fear lies more than they fear being outflanked in a debate. We must fear misrepresentation more than we fear losing a point. We must fear turning truth into propaganda, because propaganda is always tempted to sacrifice reality for effect.

Testing everything without becoming suspicious of everything

Paul's command in 1 Thessalonians is brief and bracing: "Test everything; hold fast what is good" (1 Thessalonians 5:21, RSV). This line is sometimes used to justify endless skepticism or spiritual restlessness. But that is not what Paul is doing. He is describing a mature posture: a willingness to examine claims, to discern what is consistent with the Gospel, and to keep what is genuinely good.

This is deeply relevant online because the internet is a factory of claims. Some are true, some are half-true, some are distortions, and some are malicious. Christians must not be gullible. "Test everything" means we do not repeat rumors because they fit our narrative. We do not accept accusations because they flatter our bias. We do not amplify claims simply because they are emotionally satisfying. We examine. We verify. We compare sources. We check context. We ask whether something is credible. Then—and only then—do we speak.

At the same time, "hold fast what is good" means we are not allowed to become cynics. Cynicism feels like wisdom online, but it often becomes a spiritual poison. A Christian who is suspicious of everything can lose gratitude, hope, and the ability to recognize genuine goodness in people who are not "on our side." Paul commands both testing and holding fast. Discernment is not the same as distrust.

Humility across traditions without relativism

One of the most difficult and necessary disciplines for online Christian influencers is learning across traditions without falling into either arrogance or relativism. Online culture loves tribes. It rewards the posture that says, "We have the truth; everyone else is compromised." It also rewards, in other circles, a shallow tolerance that says, "All views are basically the same; nothing really matters." Both postures fail the Gospel.

Christian humility means acknowledging that no individual Christian sees everything clearly, and no tradition is immune to blind spots. Even within the Church, believers grow over time. We learn. We repent. We refine language. We recover neglected truths. We correct distortions. The history of doctrine itself reveals that the Church has often had to speak more carefully over time, not because truth changes, but because human understanding needs purification.

At the same time, humility is not relativism. Humility does not mean treating contradiction as harmless. The Gospel contains claims that are either true or false. Christ is either risen or not. God either reveals himself or does not. Sin either destroys or it does not. The Christian can learn across traditions precisely because he believes God is the author of truth and therefore truth can be recognized, received, and honored wherever it is found. To learn from someone outside your tradition is not to surrender your convictions; it is to practice gratitude for God's gifts.

A mature online witness can therefore say two things at once: "I am committed to the truth God has revealed," and "I am still learning, and I may be corrected." That combination is rare online. It is also powerful.

Formation and competence: loving your audience enough to be careful

To speak publicly about God requires a certain competence. Not the competence of being a professional scholar, but the competence of being responsible. Online ministry can make us forget this because it feels informal. But the moral weight remains. When you teach, you are shaping souls.

Competence begins with the humility to study. It includes learning to read Scripture in context, to avoid twisting passages into slogans, to distinguish central doctrines from secondary matters, and to recognize when a topic requires patience rather than speed. It also includes the willingness to say, "I don't know," which is one of the most truthful sentences a Christian can speak. The desire to appear knowledgeable is one of the easiest ways to become careless with truth.

Competence also includes learning how to verify claims before repeating them. It means resisting "screenshot theology" and "headline theology." It means not building arguments on rumors. It means distinguishing evidence from interpretation. And when you do make a mistake, competence means correcting it quickly and plainly, because love of truth is stronger than love of ego.

In short, loving truth is part of loving neighbor. The people who listen to you deserve more than your instinct. They deserve your care.

The freedom truth gives

Jesus promises that truth makes us free (John 8:32). In online life, freedom often looks like not being manipulated by trends, outrage cycles, and tribal pressure. It looks like being able to refuse a narrative that your group demands, because reality is more important than belonging. It looks like being able to correct yourself without feeling that your identity is collapsing. It looks like being able to honor what is good in others without fear of disloyalty.

Truth also frees us from the exhausting performance of certainty. The Christian witness does not have to pretend to be omniscient. She can be honest about what she knows, careful about what she doesn't, and courageous about what she must proclaim. That honesty itself becomes a form of credibility in a world built on exaggeration.

To know the truth, then, is not merely to stockpile information. It is to cultivate a truthful soul—formed by Christ's word, disciplined by careful thinking, humble enough to learn, and courageous enough to hold fast to what is good.

Discussion Questions

1. In your online habits, are you more tempted toward arrogance ("I already know") or toward relativism ("it doesn't really matter")? Why?

2. When was the last time you publicly corrected yourself? What emotions did that stir—shame, fear, freedom, gratitude?

3. Do you tend to "test everything" with careful discernment, or do you slide into cynicism and suspicion? How can you tell the difference in yourself?

4. What practices would help you love truth more than winning—slower posting, deeper study, better verification, more prayer, stronger accountability?

5. How might your content change if Philippians 4:8 shaped your mind more than the platform's outrage incentives?

Closing Prayer

Lord Jesus Christ, you have promised that if we continue in your word, we will know the truth, and the truth will make us free. Deliver me from careless speech, from the performance of certainty, and from the temptation to use truth as a weapon. Give me a mind disciplined to dwell on what is true, honorable, just, pure, lovely, and gracious. Teach me to test everything with discernment and to hold fast what is good. Make me humble enough to learn, courageous enough to confess what is true, and faithful enough to correct myself when I err, so that my witness may serve your discipleship and glorify your Name. Amen.

Chapter 8

Controversy, Straw Men, and the Duty of Fairness

Online platforms thrive on controversy. They reward conflict because conflict keeps attention locked in place. A calm, careful explanation may help a soul, but it rarely triggers the surge of engagement that an argument will. Outrage spreads faster than nuance. Mockery travels farther than patient reasoning. In that environment, Christian influencers face a constant moral pressure: to speak in ways that win the moment rather than in ways that tell the truth.

This pressure affects not only our tone but also our honesty. It is easy to "win" online by attacking an opponent's weakest version, by selecting the least articulate representative of a view, or by summarizing a complex position in a way that makes it obviously ridiculous. This is the practice commonly called building a "straw man"—constructing a simplified, distorted version of someone's belief so that you can knock it down. A straw man feels like courage, especially when your audience applauds. But Scripture treats this as a failure of wisdom and a failure of love.

If we are going to speak publicly as Christians, we must accept a duty that is both moral and evangelistic: the duty of fairness. We must refuse caricature, even when caricature is profitable. We must learn to represent other views accurately, even when accuracy makes the argument harder. And we must correct error without contempt, because the goal is not humiliation but truth and, where possible, conversion.

The platform temptation in this chapter: content "built to dunk"

Many forms of online content are designed primarily to produce a "dunk." The creator frames an opponent as obviously foolish, selects an extreme clip, adds sarcasm, and delivers a punchline. The audience laughs, shares, and feels confirmed. The creator grows. The platform rewards the heat. The cycle repeats.

But a dunk rarely persuades the person being dunked on, and it rarely forms mature disciples. It forms spectators who crave another win. It trains Christians to enjoy contempt. It also trains them to substitute performance for truth. Over time, the creator can become addicted to the role of conqueror and unable to speak in any other register. Even when the creator's conclusions are correct, the method can be spiritually damaging.

Christians must be willing to lose engagement in order to keep integrity. If your influence depends on misrepresenting others, it is not Christian influence. It is propaganda with religious language.

The wisdom of hearing before answering

Proverbs names one of the most common online sins with surgical precision: "If one gives answer before he hears, it is his folly and shame" (Proverbs 18:13, RSV). Online culture encourages this folly. It rewards fast reaction. It rewards commentary before comprehension. It rewards the quick retort that signals confidence, even if it is based on misunderstanding.

But Scripture calls this shameful. Before you respond, you must hear. That means you must actually understand what the other person is claiming, why they believe it, and what their best reasons are. In many online disputes, people are not even disagreeing about the same thing; they are reacting to a caricature of what they think the other person meant. Proverbs exposes that as folly.

"Hearing" also means resisting the desire to interpret the other person in the worst possible light. Online platforms often train us into a hermeneutic of suspicion: we assume bad motives, assume the worst meaning, and then respond to that assumption with heat. But Christian fairness begins by asking, "What is the strongest, most coherent form of what they are trying to say?" Only then can you address it honestly.

"Quick to hear, slow to speak"

James deepens the moral discipline required for controversy: "Let every man be quick to hear, slow to speak, slow to anger" (James 1:19, RSV). This verse is not simply advice for polite conversation. It is a spiritual rule for online engagement. It calls you to slow down in exactly the places where the platform wants you to speed up.

To be "quick to hear" online means you pause before replying, you read carefully, you watch the full clip rather than the edited snippet, you consult primary sources rather than summaries, and you ask clarifying questions when something is ambiguous. To be "slow to speak" means you do not treat every provocation as a summons. You do not comment simply because you can. You do not post while emotionally heated. You allow time for prayer, for verification, and for self-examination.

To be "slow to anger" does not mean you never feel righteous indignation. Scripture recognizes that anger can arise in the presence of genuine injustice. But James warns that anger is spiritually hazardous, because anger quickly becomes a license for exaggeration and contempt. The internet trains us to live at a constant simmer. James calls us to a different spirit.

The Christian duty to "steel-man" rather than straw-man

If straw-manning is distorting an opponent's view to make it easier to defeat, steel-manning is the opposite: presenting an opponent's view in its strongest reasonable form so that you can engage it honestly. This practice is not merely intellectual virtue. It is Christian charity applied to argument.

Steel-manning does not require you to agree. It requires you to be fair. It means you ask, "Who are the most serious thinkers in this tradition? What do they actually claim? What are their strongest texts, arguments, and experiences? How would they state their position if they were trying to be precise?" Then you respond to that.

This approach does two things at once. First, it protects truth, because it reduces the chance that you are arguing against something imaginary. Second, it protects your witness, because it signals to outsiders that Christianity is not afraid of serious engagement. It shows that you are not trying to win by distortion. And when you do disagree, your disagreement will sound more credible because you have demonstrated that you understand what you are rejecting.

If you cannot state the other side's view in a way they would recognize as fair, you are not ready to refute it.

Giving a defense with gentleness and reverence

Peter instructs Christians on how to speak in contested environments: "Always be prepared to make a defense to any one who calls you to account for the hope that is in you, yet do it with gentleness and reverence; and keep your conscience clear" (1 Peter 3:15–16, RSV). This passage is often quoted as a mandate for apologetics, and it is. But it is also a mandate for tone and method.

Peter assumes Christians will face questions and objections. He expects us to be prepared. That preparation implies study and competence. But Peter also insists that defense must be offered "with gentleness and reverence." Gentleness is not timidity; it is strength under control. Reverence means you remember you are speaking before God about matters that touch souls. You do not treat sacred truth as a tool for entertainment. You do not treat opponents as objects.

Peter then adds a crucial phrase: "keep your conscience clear." A clear conscience in online controversy means you did not cheat. You did not distort. You did not conceal key facts. You did not weaponize rumors. You did not use sarcasm to avoid substance. You did not attack a person when you could not answer an argument. You told the truth as you understood it, you spoke with charity, and you were willing to be corrected if you misunderstood.

This is one of the hidden marks of mature Christian influence: you can disagree strongly and still keep your conscience clear.

Why fairness is evangelistically wise

Fairness is not only a moral duty; it is evangelistically wise. Many unbelievers assume Christians are either ignorant or manipulative. Many have encountered only shallow caricatures of their own views coming from religious voices. When a Christian demonstrates careful listening and accurate representation, it disarms suspicion. It does not guarantee agreement, but it opens the possibility of real conversation.

Fairness also protects unity among Christians. Many intra-Christian conflicts online are intensified by straw-manning. People interpret one another in the worst possible light, and then mobilize their audiences against one another. The result is scandal: outsiders see Christians devouring each other and conclude that the Gospel is not real. Peter's insistence on gentleness and reverence matters here. If Christians cannot speak to one another with fairness, why would outsiders trust us to speak about God?

A practical posture for controversy

Not every controversy deserves your attention. A platform trains you to treat every provocation as content. Wisdom teaches you to discern. Before engaging, ask whether you can add light rather than heat, whether your audience will be formed toward charity, and whether your own heart is calm enough to speak truthfully. Sometimes the most faithful act is to be silent, to pray, and to refuse to feed the outrage machine.

When you do engage, aim for clarity rather than victory. Say what you mean. Define terms. Cite primary sources when possible. Acknowledge complexity where it exists. Give credit where it is due. Admit when the other side has a legitimate concern or a point worth hearing. Then state your disagreement plainly and without contempt.

This is slower. It is less entertaining. It may even cost you engagement. But it is far more likely to produce disciples who love truth and love neighbor.

In a world built to reward caricature, the Christian who refuses straw men becomes a sign of a different Kingdom.

Discussion Questions

1. When you feel the urge to respond to controversy online, is it usually driven by love of truth and neighbor, or by adrenaline and the desire to "win"?

2. Can you accurately state the best version of a view you strongly oppose? What would you need to read or watch to do that fairly?

3. How often do you answer before you truly hear (Proverbs 18:13)? What habits would slow you down in a healthy way?

4. What would "gentleness and reverence" look like in your tone, your captions, and your comment replies (1 Peter 3:15)?

5. Is there a controversy you should step away from—not because truth doesn't matter, but because the platform is shaping you toward anger and contempt?

Closing Prayer

Lord Jesus Christ, you are the Truth, and you have commanded us to love our neighbor as ourselves. Deliver me from the desire to win by distortion and from the pleasure of humiliating others. Teach me to be quick to hear, slow to speak, and slow to anger. Give me the humility to understand before I answer and the courage to speak truthfully when I must. Grant that I may always be ready to give a defense of the hope that is in me, yet to do so with gentleness and reverence, keeping my conscience clear before you. Make my words instruments of light rather than heat, for your glory and the good of souls. Amen.

Chapter 9

We Stand Under Judgment: The Person Behind the Screen

One of the most spiritually dangerous features of online life is how easily it can make other people feel unreal. A username replaces a face. A profile picture replaces a voice. A comment replaces a story. And once a person becomes an abstraction, it becomes easier to speak harshly, to assume motives, to mock, to pile on, and to treat cruelty as if it were simply "debate."

But the person behind the screen is not an abstraction. He or she is a human being—made in the image of God, carried by a particular history, wounded in specific ways, and accountable to God in the end. The Christian cannot forget this without deforming the Gospel into something unrecognizable.

In earlier chapters we spoke about truth, fairness, and the dangers of the cult of personality. Here we arrive at a deeper moral reality that must govern all Christian speech online: **we stand under judgment**, and so does everyone we address. Christian online ministry is not merely public communication. It is moral action, performed before God, touching souls, and leaving traces that may last far longer than the moment.

Jesus warns us not only that judgment is real, but that our own habits of judgment shape the standard by which we will be judged: "With the judgment you pronounce you will be judged, and the measure you give will be the measure you get" (Matthew 7:2, RSV). This does not mean Christians never discern or never correct. It means we must remember who we are when we speak: not gods, not final arbiters, not owners of other people's souls, but sinners who will answer for our words.

Paul makes the same point with even greater directness: "Why do you pass judgment on your brother? Or you, why do you despise your brother? For we shall all stand before the judgment seat of God… So each of us shall give account of himself to God" (Romans 14:10–12, RSV). The apostle does not treat contempt as a small problem. He places it under the shadow of the judgment seat. He reminds Christians that the person we are tempted to despise is our brother—or at least a neighbor for whom Christ died—and that despising another is incompatible with living in the fear of God.

And Jesus gives the most sobering lens of all for how we treat others: "As you did it to one of the least of these my brethren, you did it to me" (Matthew 25:40, RSV). Online life often tempts us to think that our words are aimed at "ideas." But our words always land on persons. When we humiliate a person, we train our hearts toward contempt. When we speak truth without mercy, we train our hearts toward hardness. And Jesus says that how we treat the vulnerable is a measure of how we are treating him.

The platform temptation in this chapter: heat that dehumanizes

Platforms are designed to intensify emotions. They reward what provokes reaction, and reaction is often strongest when a person feels threatened, insulted, or morally outraged. Over time, this environment can train Christians to live in a permanent state of heat. Not righteous zeal, but something closer to irritability and suspicion. The soul becomes keyed to conflict. The mind begins to interpret disagreement as danger. The heart becomes quick to condemn and slow to understand.

This is where dehumanization grows. A person becomes "the enemy," "the heretic," "the woke one," "the trad one," "the lib," "the fundamentalist," "the idiot," "the fraud." Once reduced to a label, they no longer require patience. They no longer deserve careful listening. They become a target.

Christians must recognize this as a spiritual threat. The Gospel cannot be proclaimed by contempt without being distorted. Even when we are addressing genuine error, the person remains a person. If we forget that, we may win arguments and lose souls—including our own.

Moral injury: what online cruelty does to the speaker

There is another dimension Christians must acknowledge: harsh online behavior does not only harm the recipient; it harms the speaker. Repeatedly speaking with contempt, mockery, and cruelty creates a kind of moral injury. It dulls the conscience. It makes sin feel normal. It teaches the heart to enjoy humiliation. It trains the mind to interpret other people as obstacles rather than neighbors.

Many creators discover this only after years. They realize they are angrier than they used to be. They are less patient, less gentle, more reactive, and more suspicious. They pray less. They rest less. They enjoy "wins" more than they enjoy mercy. The platform may call this strength. Scripture calls it a danger to the soul.

This is why Romans 14 is so important. Paul does not merely say, "Try to be nice." He says, "We shall all stand before the judgment seat of God." The Christian must speak online with a conscience shaped by eternity. Your audience is not merely your audience;

they are people who will stand before God. And you will also stand before God, accountable for how you treated them.

Mercy without surrendering truth

At this point, many Christians fear that emphasizing mercy will lead to compromise. They worry that to speak gently is to become vague, and to refuse contempt is to refuse clarity. But Scripture does not allow that false choice. Mercy is not the opposite of truth; mercy is the manner in which truth is meant to be spoken and applied.

Jesus himself speaks hard truths. He calls sin what it is. He warns of judgment. He confronts hypocrisy. Yet he also welcomes sinners, eats with them, and offers forgiveness. He does not treat people as disposable. He does not use their failure as entertainment. His severity is never the playful cruelty of a performer; it is the serious mercy of a physician. He wants repentance, not humiliation. He wants salvation, not spectacle.

Christian online ministry must aim for the same posture. There are real errors to correct. There are real injustices to name. There are real dangers to warn against. But the Christian does not speak as one who despises. The Christian speaks as one who fears God, loves neighbor, and remembers his own need for mercy.

Romans 14 helps here because it exposes not only judgment but contempt: "Why do you despise your brother?" (Romans 14:10). Contempt is more than disagreement. It is a heart posture that says, "You are beneath me." Contempt is a way of viewing another person as unworthy of dignity. A Christian can refute an argument without contempt. A Christian can name a sin without contempt. A Christian can warn against error without contempt. The moment contempt enters, the spirit of Christ has been displaced.

Seeing Christ in the "least"

Matthew 25:40 pushes this even further by tying our treatment of others to our treatment of Christ: "As you did it to one of the least of these my brethren, you did it to me." Online life makes it easy to ignore the "least." The "least" may be the person who is confused, poorly educated, emotionally reactive, or socially awkward. The "least" may be the one who comments clumsily or asks naïve questions. The "least" may be the one whose pain shows through in sarcasm.

The Christian creator is often tempted to use such people as examples—screenshots for ridicule, cautionary tales for "content," or public lessons delivered with humiliation. But Jesus tells us that the way we treat the least is a measure of how we are treating him. That should sober us. It should also re-humanize the comment section. Your audience is not a feed; it is a collection of souls. Some are strong. Many are weak. Some are sincere. Some are hostile. Some are wounded. Christ sees them all.

This does not mean you let abusive behavior continue without boundaries. Mercy is not permissiveness. A Christian can set limits, block harassment, and refuse to engage bad-faith provocations. But even boundaries should be set without cruelty. The Christian can say "no" without hate.

Practicing a different kind of online presence

If we truly believe we stand under judgment, our online behavior will change. We will become slower to condemn and quicker to ask questions. We will avoid making snap conclusions about someone's motives. We will resist pile-ons, because mob behavior is rarely righteous. We will refuse to use humiliation as entertainment. We will be willing to disengage when the conversation is producing more heat than light.

We will also cultivate the habit of remembering the person behind the screen. Before replying, it can help to imagine the other person sitting across from you in a room, with a real face, a real history, and a real vulnerability. Many things we would never say in person are said online because we forget that we are speaking to a human being. Christians must fight that forgetfulness.

And we will practice mercy not as weakness but as obedience. The Christian is free to speak truth because the Christian is not trying to dominate. The Christian is free to be gentle because the Christian does not need to perform strength. The Christian is free to correct without contempt because the Christian remembers that he too will be judged.

What will we answer for?

Romans 14 ends with a simple, terrifying statement: "So each of us shall give account of himself to God" (Romans 14:12). You will not give account for how many followers you gained. You will not give account for whether your "dunks" were praised. You will give account for whether you spoke truthfully, whether you loved your neighbor, whether you guarded your tongue, whether you cultivated contempt, whether you harmed the vulnerable, and whether you pointed people toward Christ.

If that is true—and it is—then the person behind the screen becomes holy ground. Not because every opinion is sacred, but because every person is someone for whom Christ died, someone who will stand before God, someone whom you are commanded to love. When Christians remember this, the tone of online witness becomes different. It becomes less performative and more reverent. It becomes less tribal and more humane. It becomes less addicted to heat and more committed to holiness.

We stand under judgment. That is not meant to paralyze us. It is meant to purify us.

Discussion Questions

1. When you read a comment that irritates you, what happens first in your heart—curiosity, anger, fear, or contempt? What does that reveal?

2. How might your online tone change if you remembered daily that you will stand before the judgment seat of God (Romans 14:10)?

3. Are there certain "types" of people you find easy to dehumanize online? Why? What labels do you tend to use?

4. Where is the line for you between setting boundaries and speaking with cruelty? How can you enforce boundaries without contempt?

5. Can you recall a time when harsh Christian speech online pushed someone away from the Gospel? What might mercy with truth have looked like instead?

Closing Prayer

Lord Jesus Christ, Judge of the living and the dead, set your fear in my heart—not fear that drives me to harshness, but fear that purifies my speech. Deliver me from contempt, from dehumanizing those you have made, and from the heat that turns neighbors into enemies. Teach me to remember the person behind the screen and to see your image in them. Give me courage to speak truthfully and the grace to speak mercifully, so that my words may heal rather than wound. Keep my conscience clear before you, for I too will give account to God. Amen.

Chapter 10

Speech That Heals: Rebuke Without Contempt

Online spaces have made speech cheap. Words can be fired off instantly, in public, and with little sense of consequence. We can speak harshly, and if we feel guilty, we can justify ourselves by saying we were "just telling the truth." We can mock, and excuse it as "humor." We can label someone an idiot, and call it "discernment." We can publicly humiliate a person, and baptize it as "accountability." The platform then rewards the harshness with engagement, and the cycle repeats.

But Scripture treats words as morally serious. Words are not merely expressions of personality; they are instruments that can bless or curse, heal or harm, build up or tear down. This is especially true when we speak in Christ's name. Christian speech is never only about being correct. It is also about being Christlike. And Christlike correction does not rely on contempt.

Jesus issues one of the most sobering warnings about contemptuous speech: "Whoever says, 'You fool!' shall be liable to the hell of fire" (Matthew 5:22, RSV). He is not policing vocabulary like an etiquette teacher. He is exposing a spiritual reality: contempt is a form of violence. It treats another person as beneath dignity. It denies, in practice, that the other is a neighbor made in God's image. And once contempt is tolerated, cruelty becomes easy.

That is why a Christian who wants to evangelize online must learn a discipline that feels almost impossible in the attention economy: **rebuke without contempt**. We must learn how to correct as a physician heals—truthfully, carefully, and for the sake of restoration—rather than as an executioner punishes.

The platform temptation in this chapter: spiritual violence disguised as courage

Online culture often equates harshness with strength. It praises the one who is "brutally honest." It rewards the voice that cuts and humiliates. It tells Christians that if they soften their tone, they are compromising truth. This is a dangerous lie. Cruelty is not courage. Contempt is not clarity. Humiliation is not holiness.

The temptation becomes even stronger when we are dealing with genuine sin, real injustice, or destructive teaching. In those moments, anger feels justified, and the platform offers a ready-made script: expose, denounce, mock, and rally the crowd. The problem is that crowd-rallying often becomes its own reward. The creator enjoys the sense of power, and the audience enjoys the sense of superiority. Meanwhile, the person being addressed is rarely led to repentance. More often they are hardened, shamed, or pushed into deeper defensiveness. What looked like zeal becomes spiritual violence.

Christian correction must ask a different question: not merely "Is this wrong?" but "How will my words affect the soul I am addressing, and the souls watching?" If your rebuke produces only humiliation and rage, it is not healing speech—even if the underlying point was true.

"Let no evil talk come out of your mouths"

Paul sets a standard for Christian communication that is both simple and demanding: "Let no evil talk come out of your mouths, but only such as is good for edifying, as fits the occasion, that it may impart grace to those who hear" (Ephesians 4:29, RSV). The criterion is not whether your words feel satisfying to say. The criterion is whether they build up and impart grace.

This does not mean Christian speech is always soft. Sometimes building up requires warning, correction, and clear naming of sin. But even warning must be ordered toward grace. If the goal is to destroy a person's dignity, you are not imparting grace. If the goal is to score points, you are not edifying. If the tone is contempt, the speech is already corrupt, because contempt cannot impart grace.

Paul's phrase "as fits the occasion" matters too. The same words can be appropriate in one context and harmful in another. A strong rebuke might be necessary in a private pastoral situation but scandalous in a public pile-on. A sharp warning might be needed to protect the vulnerable, but it must still be framed in a way that calls people toward Christ rather than toward hatred.

This is what makes online speech so difficult: the occasion is often unclear. The audience is mixed. The vulnerable are listening. The scrupulous are listening. The wounded are listening. The proud are listening. And the creator is tempted to speak for applause rather than for edification.

The Lord's servant and the art of correction

Paul's pastoral counsel to Timothy is especially suited to the digital age: "The Lord's servant must not be quarrelsome but kindly to every one, an apt teacher, forbearing, correcting his opponents with gentleness. God may perhaps grant that they will repent and come to know the truth" (2 Timothy 2:24–25, RSV). Here we find a whole theology of correction in a few lines.

First, the Lord's servant "must not be quarrelsome." That is devastating to the online persona that thrives on constant fights. It does not say the Lord's servant never argues; it says he is not quarrelsome. Quarrelsome means eager for dispute, addicted to contention, constantly needing to respond. A quarrelsome spirit is not a mark of faithfulness. It is a spiritual disorder.

Second, the Lord's servant is to be "kindly to every one." This is not sentimental. It includes opponents. It includes those who misunderstand you. It includes those who irritate you. Kindness is not weakness. It is the disciplined refusal to treat people as disposable.

Third, the Lord's servant corrects "with gentleness." Gentleness here is not cowardice. It is controlled strength. It is the ability to speak clearly without becoming cruel. Gentleness also protects truth, because it keeps you from exaggeration and from the distortions that anger produces.

Finally, Paul locates repentance where it belongs: in God's gift. "God may perhaps grant that they will repent and come to know the truth." This sentence rescues the Christian corrector from the savior-complex. You are not converting people by force. You are not humiliating them into holiness. You are speaking truthfully and gently, praying that God will grant repentance. That posture changes everything. It makes correction less theatrical and more prayerful. It shifts the goal from "winning" to "restoring."

Nathan's parable: conviction without humiliation

Scripture also gives us a masterclass in how to convict without contempt in the story of Nathan and David. After David's grave sin, Nathan does not begin by screaming accusations. He tells a parable: a rich man with many flocks steals the single beloved lamb of a poor man and kills it for a guest (2 Samuel 12). David burns with anger at the injustice and pronounces judgment. Only then does Nathan deliver the piercing words: "You are the man" (2 Samuel 12:7).

Nathan's method matters. He leads David to recognize evil as evil before David recognizes it in himself. He bypasses David's defenses by engaging David's moral imagination. The goal is not to crush David for sport, but to awaken David to repentance. Nathan does not deny the seriousness of sin; he reveals it in a way that makes repentance possible.

Online correction often fails because it goes straight to humiliation. It attacks the person's identity publicly and makes repentance psychologically difficult. A humiliated person usually becomes defensive. Nathan shows another way: speak truth that penetrates, not truth that performs. Speak in a way that allows the conscience to awaken rather than forcing the ego to defend itself.

This does not mean every online correction must be parabolic storytelling. It means Christian correction should aim at **conviction rather than contempt**, and conviction often requires wisdom about how humans actually respond.

Correcting as a physician, not an executioner

A physician names a disease clearly, but does so to heal the patient. An executioner names a crime and seeks punishment. Online Christian speech often drifts into executioner mode because executioner speech is thrilling. It makes the speaker feel powerful. It excites the crowd. It produces engagement. And it gives the illusion of holiness without the cost of mercy.

But the Gospel calls Christians to be agents of reconciliation. Even when discipline is necessary, even when warnings are urgent, even when scandal must be addressed, the Christian must remember the purpose: repentance, restoration, and the protection of the vulnerable. An executioner seeks destruction. A physician seeks healing.

Practically, this means the Christian corrector must learn to separate the person from the sin without pretending sin is harmless. It means we refuse name-calling, mockery, and contempt. It means we speak with a gravity appropriate to souls. It means we are willing to say hard things without enjoying them.

And it means we pay attention to how our speech forms our audience. If your followers learn to mock and pile on, your ministry is forming them into something other than disciples.

When strong words are necessary

Some Christians will object: did Jesus not speak strongly? Did he not call some leaders "hypocrites"? Yes. Scripture contains strong prophetic speech. But even that speech is not a license for contempt. Jesus' severity is never mere insult. It is truth spoken with holy purpose. It aims to reveal, to warn, and to call to repentance. It is not entertainment. It is not branding. And it is not the default mode of his ministry.

A Christian influencer should therefore be cautious about imitating the sharpest moments of Jesus while ignoring his patient, merciful, and often quietly invitational manner. Strong words may be necessary at times, but they must be anchored in prayer, moral seriousness, and a genuine desire for the other's good—not in the thrill of being applauded for harshness.

Discussion Questions

1. When you feel justified anger online, how often does it lead you toward contempt? What does that do to your heart over time?

2. Do your words tend to "impart grace to those who hear" (Ephesians 4:29), or do they mainly energize your audience against an enemy?

3. In your online disagreements, are you becoming quarrelsome—or are you learning to correct with gentleness (2 Timothy 2:24–25)?

4. How might Nathan's approach (2 Samuel 12) reshape the way you address sin and error—especially when others are watching?

5. What would change if you saw yourself as a physician of souls rather than as an executioner of opponents?

Closing Prayer

Lord Jesus Christ, Word made flesh, set a guard over my tongue and purify my heart. Deliver me from contempt, from harshness that wounds, and from the temptation to use truth as a weapon. Teach me to speak only what is good for edifying, fitting the occasion, that it may impart grace to those who hear. Make me a servant who is not quarrelsome, but kind, patient, and able to teach, correcting with gentleness and reverence. Grant that my words may lead to repentance and healing, not to humiliation and rage, for your glory and the salvation of souls. Amen.

Chapter 11

Prayer as the Engine of Theology: Doxology First

The digital world loves content. Content is king. It is what drives the platforms, what fills the feeds, what produces the likes, shares, and views. Christian content, in particular, often thrives on debates, arguments, and explanations. A well-crafted video or blog post can draw attention to theological truths, deliver insightful commentary, and inspire many. But in the midst of all this, we can forget that **content is not the source of theology**—prayer is. Theology is not just about ideas to be discussed; it is about a living relationship with God, and that relationship begins in prayer.

Jesus' disciples knew this instinctively. When they asked him to teach them to pray, it was because they understood that prayer was not merely a ritual or a routine; it was the core of spiritual life, the very soil in which all theology is rooted. In response to their request, Jesus gives them the Lord's Prayer, which begins not with doctrine, but with worship: "Father, hallowed be your name" (Luke 11:1, RSV). Theology, the study of God, starts with awe, reverence, and adoration. It begins with recognizing God as God—glorious, holy, and beyond our understanding.

Christian theology that is not anchored in prayer is a theology that risks becoming dry, detached, and self-referential. It risks becoming a product to be consumed rather than a living encounter with the living God. Prayer is the engine of theology because it keeps us grounded in the one who is the source of all truth. Without prayer, theology becomes speculative, impersonal, and ultimately fruitless. But when prayer and worship are the foundation, all theology becomes a response to God's revelation, a humble act of discernment, and an invitation to participate in the life of the Trinity.

The platform temptation in this chapter: content as the idol of Christian life

Online, it is easy to slip into the belief that **content** is the measure of a Christian's life and faithfulness. The platform values speed. It values novelty. It values visibility. The pressure is always there to produce more—more videos, more posts, more followers. This pressure turns theology into a commodity: something to be marketed, consumed, and moved quickly. The danger is that in the rush to create content, we forget why we create in the first place. We forget that the content we create is meant to lead people into communion with God, not replace it.

When content replaces communion with God, we create a performance, not a witness. We offer knowledge without wisdom. We offer arguments without prayer. We speak about God without actually speaking to God. In a world obsessed with content creation, it is easy to forget that the heart of Christian life is worship and prayer, not the next viral post. It is not enough to "know" the right things about God. We must also **know God**—and knowing God begins in prayer.

Prayer as the source of discernment

In the life of a Christian creator, **prayer is the source of discernment**. Discernment is not just the ability to distinguish between right and wrong, but the deeper wisdom of knowing how to speak truth in a way that builds up, heals, and leads others closer to God. Discernment comes from God, and it comes through prayer.

Paul makes this connection clear when he writes to the Romans: "I appeal to you therefore, brethren, by the mercies of God, to present your bodies as a living sacrifice, holy and acceptable to God, which is your spiritual worship" (Romans 12:1, RSV). The key here is that the **sacrifice** of our bodies, our thoughts, and our will is an act of worship. And this worship—this offering—is the foundation of Christian discernment. It is through prayer and sacrifice that our minds are transformed: "Do not be conformed to this world, but be transformed by the renewal of your mind, that you may prove what is the will of God, what is good and acceptable and perfect" (Romans 12:2, RSV).

This is how prayer leads to discernment. Through prayer, we are **transformed**. We begin to see the world through God's eyes, and we begin to recognize His will in our speech, our actions, and our decisions. When we are not rooted in prayer, we cannot hope to make the right decisions because our perspective becomes clouded by our own desires and the distractions of the world. But when prayer is the center, we can approach all things with God's wisdom, rather than our own.

In online spaces, this means that Christian creators must resist the temptation to produce content simply for the sake of engagement or controversy. Instead, they must discern, through prayer, whether what they are creating is truly serving the purposes of God. Is it contributing to the Kingdom? Is it building people up in love? Is it drawing people closer to God? Prayer is the filter through which we evaluate every piece of content we create.

Worship as the highest theology

Christian theology begins in prayer and ends in prayer. If theology is simply a set of doctrines, it is incomplete. Theology must always be a response to God's self-revelation, and this response is worship. Worship is the highest form of theology because it recognizes that all theology points to God—not just to ideas, but to the living God.

Paul's letter to the Colossians illustrates this beautifully: "Let the word of Christ dwell in you richly, teaching and admonishing one another in all wisdom, singing psalms and hymns and spiritual songs, with thankfulness in your hearts to God. And whatever you do, in word or deed, do everything in the name of the Lord Jesus, giving thanks to God the Father through him" (Colossians 3:16–17, RSV). Here, Paul connects **teaching** and **worship**: the word of Christ is not merely something to be understood, but something to be lived, sung, and rejoiced in. Theology that does not result in worship is not complete theology. It is intellectualism. It is pride.

Worship brings the truth to life. It makes the truth personal. Worship is the **response to truth**, the way in which our minds, hearts, and lives are aligned with God's will. This is why worship is the highest form of theology: it is where we fully acknowledge God as the center of our lives and the source of all truth.

When prayer is the engine of theology, our theological understanding becomes an act of worship, not a tool for division or self-aggrandizement. The goal is not to be right or to win debates. The goal is to bring God glory. In every piece of content we create, we must ask: Is this an act of worship? Does this reflect my love for God? Is this a humble offering that points others to Christ?

Resisting "content replaces communion with God"

One of the most subtle dangers of the digital age is that **content creation can replace communion with God**. The pressure to stay visible, to stay relevant, to keep producing can wear down even the most faithful creators. Content becomes the focus of the

Christian life. Prayer, however, is the **foundation of everything**. Without prayer, content becomes empty, performative, and spiritually dry.

Jesus understood the priority of prayer in a way that stands in stark contrast to the demands of the modern world. In Luke 11:1, His disciples asked Him to teach them how to pray, recognizing that prayer was at the center of His life. Jesus responded with the Lord's Prayer, giving them a simple but profound model that begins with worship: "Father, hallowed be your name" (Luke 11:2, RSV). This prayer does not begin with a list of requests or a call to action; it begins with **worship**. Jesus shows us that the foundation of every word, every thought, and every action is first and foremost worship. Theology flows from this place of reverence and awe.

The Christian creator must make prayer the starting point, not just a footnote. Before we post, before we record, before we write, we must pray. We must seek God's presence, asking for His wisdom and guidance. Without prayer, content becomes a chore. With prayer, content becomes a ministry.

The gift of discernment in prayer

The more we pray, the more we are aligned with God's heart. Through prayer, we are granted the gift of discernment, allowing us to recognize what is good and true, and what is misleading or harmful. Prayer trains our hearts to be attuned to God's voice, not just the voices of the crowd or the algorithms. Through prayer, we develop a sensitivity to God's will, enabling us to act in ways that glorify Him, rather than promoting ourselves.

As Christian creators, we are called to produce content that is faithful to God's truth, but we cannot do so effectively without first **being** with God. Prayer is not only the source of discernment, but the **source of strength**. When we neglect prayer, we are left to rely on our own strength, which is fleeting. But when we pray, we are invited into the flow of God's power and wisdom, which never runs dry.

Discussion Questions

1. How often do you pause to pray before creating content, and how might that change the way you approach your work?

2. What does it mean to you that theology begins in worship and prayer, rather than in arguments or content creation?

3. How can you resist the temptation to make content creation the focus of your Christian life, rather than a form of worship?

4. Do you ever struggle with discerning what is God's will for your online work? How might prayer help in this process?

5. When you are tempted to speak or post out of frustration or pride, how can prayer help you re-align with God's will?

Closing Prayer

Father, you are the source of all truth, and we offer our minds, our words, and our work to you in worship. Forgive us for the times when we have allowed content creation to replace communion with you. Teach us to be rooted in prayer, so that all that we create reflects your wisdom and love. May our theology be shaped by your Spirit, and may our words impart grace to those who hear. Help us to serve you in all things, not for applause, but for your glory. May our content always point back to you, the author of truth. Amen.

Chapter 12

Under Authority: Correction, Accountability, and Communion

One of the easiest ways to become spiritually unsafe online is to become spiritually unaccountable. Platforms reward the lone voice: the independent truth-teller who "answers to no one," the prophet who claims to see what everyone else refuses to see, the creator who frames every criticism as persecution. Even when the message is orthodox, the posture can become distorted. The audience begins to treat the creator as the final authority, the creator begins to treat his or her own instincts as unquestionable, and Christian discipleship quietly becomes loyalty to a personality rather than obedience to Christ.

But Christianity is not designed to be lived that way. The New Testament assumes that Christian life is communal and ordered. It assumes pastors, elders, councils, correction, and mutual responsibility. Even apostles received correction. Even great leaders submitted to discernment. The Church is a body, not a cluster of solo brands.

If online Christian work is to remain faithful, it must be practiced **under authority**—not as a denial of conscience, but as a protection for the soul and a safeguard for the community. Authority, rightly understood, is meant to serve communion rather than control. It is meant to preserve the integrity of the Gospel and to protect the vulnerable from spiritual harm. When it functions well, it is a gift. When it fails, it must be addressed truthfully and wisely, not ignored or romanticized.

The platform temptation in this chapter: "I don't need anyone"

Online life subtly trains creators to believe they do not need a Church, a pastor, or a community. They have followers. They have a "mission." They have an audience that affirms them. They can read Scripture for themselves and build content from their own conclusions. And because platforms reward confidence, a creator can begin to confuse confidence with calling.

This is dangerous because a person without accountability often becomes trapped inside his or her own blind spots. He or she may start to treat disagreement as attack. She may lose the ability to repent publicly. She may become rigid, defensive, and harsh. And without a community that knows him personally—where people can observe his character, his habits, his relationships, and his humility—he may become outwardly impressive while inwardly drifting.

Authority is not meant to crush the Christian. It is meant to keep the Christian sane.

Obedience as spiritual protection

Hebrews speaks plainly about the normal posture of believers toward their leaders: "Obey your leaders and submit to them; for they are keeping watch over your souls, as men who will have to give account" (Hebrews 13:17, RSV). This verse is often abused by authoritarian leaders, and because of that abuse, some Christians react by rejecting the concept of submission altogether. But the biblical vision is deeper and more balanced than either blind obedience or total independence.

Notice the reason Hebrews gives: leaders "are keeping watch over your souls." Authority here is pastoral. It is oriented toward care.

And leaders will "have to give account." That means leaders are not ultimate. They are responsible before God. Authority is not a private possession; it is a stewardship.

This passage also reveals why authority matters for online ministry. If someone is "keeping watch over your soul," then your online presence is not merely your project. It is part of your discipleship. You do not get to create a second spiritual life online, separate from the one you live under pastoral care. If you are called to teach and influence, you need someone who can ask hard questions, challenge your tone, correct your errors, and notice when your ministry is becoming spiritually harmful—for you or for others.

Submission, in this sense, is not humiliation. It is spiritual safety.

Correction among leaders: Paul confronts Peter

The New Testament also makes clear that authority does not eliminate correction. In Galatians, Paul describes confronting Peter: "When Cephas came to Antioch I opposed him to his face, because he stood condemned" (Galatians 2:11, RSV). The issue was not trivial. Peter's behavior—pulling back from table fellowship with Gentile believers under social pressure—communicated a false gospel in practice. Paul then explains that this behavior was "not straightforward about the truth of the gospel" (Galatians 2:14).

This episode is crucial for two reasons. First, it shows that even the most prominent leaders are not above correction. Peter is not treated as untouchable. Second, it shows how correction is meant to function in the service of the Gospel. Paul does not confront Peter to win status. He confronts him because the truth of the Gospel is at stake and because Peter's behavior is harming the Church.

For online creators, Galatians 2 exposes a common danger: confusing respect for authority with immunity from critique. It is possible to honor leaders and still recognize their errors. It is possible to submit and still speak truthfully when the Gospel is compromised. The challenge is to do this with integrity, courage, and a spirit that seeks restoration rather than humiliation.

Acts 15: discernment in communion

Acts 15 gives the Church's most foundational example of communal discernment when a major controversy threatened unity. The question was intense: must Gentile converts adopt the full yoke of Jewish law? The apostles and elders gather, arguments are heard, testimony is offered, Scripture is interpreted, and a judgment is made. Then the decision is communicated to the churches as a communal act of discernment.

This chapter is immensely important for online life, because online disputes often mimic Acts 15 in reverse. Instead of gathering, listening, weighing testimony, and seeking the Spirit's guidance, we rush to declare verdicts in public. Instead of honoring the Church's slow process of discernment, we chase outrage and demand immediate conclusions. Acts 15 reveals a different ecclesial rhythm: the Church argues, but in communion; it discerns, but with humility; it decides, but with a view to unity and pastoral care.

For creators, Acts 15 suggests that when disputes arise—especially disputes that involve doctrine, pastoral practice, or the health of the Church—the faithful response is not immediate public warfare. The faithful response is to seek counsel, listen, and submit the question to the Church's discernment rather than turning it into content.

Forms of accountability for digital missionaries

To live "under authority" does not mean every Christian must have the same structure. Traditions differ in polity, and individual circumstances differ. But the principle is consistent: Christian public ministry requires accountable relationships.

For many, this begins with being truly rooted in a local church community where you worship, serve, and are known. It also often includes some form of spiritual direction—someone mature who can help you discern motives, pray through temptations, and recognize blind spots. Peer accountability matters as well: trusted friends who can tell you when your tone has become harsh, when your content is becoming reactive, or when you are drifting into pride or exhaustion. For clergy, formal structures of oversight and canonical accountability carry particular weight. For lay creators, accountability may be less formal, but it should still be real.

The key is that correction must be possible. If no one can correct you, you are in danger.

What to do when authority fails

The difficult question is what to do when authority itself becomes unhealthy—when leaders abuse power, demand silence in the face of wrongdoing, use Scripture as a weapon, or refuse accountability themselves. Hebrews 13:17 has been misused to sanctify control. Christians who have suffered under such misuse often find it hard to trust authority again, and that fear is understandable. But the solution is not to abandon authority as such. The solution is to pursue **legitimate** authority and healthy accountability.

Galatians 2 shows that leaders can be confronted when they act "not straightforward about the truth of the gospel." Acts 15 shows that disputes can be brought into communal discernment rather than being handled privately by a single unchecked figure. Together, these passages imply several principles.

First, obedience is never a mandate to participate in sin or to cover wrongdoing. Christian submission is ordered toward God. When leaders command what God forbids, conscience must remain awake. Second, the Church's authority is meant to be shared and accountable, not concentrated without checks. When leadership becomes isolated, secretive, or immune to review, danger increases. Third, when authority fails locally, it may be necessary to seek counsel beyond the immediate setting—trusted elders, denominational structures where they exist, reputable spiritual directors, or outside authorities within one's tradition who can assist. Fourth, in cases of abuse, exploitation, or criminal behavior, protection of the vulnerable is urgent, and appropriate reporting and safeguards are necessary. The Church's duty to protect the vulnerable is not opposed to the Church's life; it is part of it.

For online creators, authority failure creates its own temptations. Some respond by making every failure into content, turning pain into a perpetual outrage machine. Others respond by silence that enables harm. Both extremes are dangerous. Wisdom seeks truth with reverence, speaks in appropriate ways, and pursues protection and reform without turning justice into performance.

Authority as communion, not control

At its healthiest, being under authority is not primarily about being managed. It is about belonging to a communion that guards the Gospel and forms the saints. When authority is exercised as service, it frees the Christian creator from the pressure of self-justification. You do not have to be the final judge of yourself. You can be corrected. You can be guided. You can be protected from your own blind spots. You can rest.

And when authority is exercised well, it also protects the audience. People who are influenced by your work can know that you are not acting as a free-floating spiritual entrepreneur. You are a member of the Church, accountable, rooted, and willing to be corrected.

Online ministry without accountability is a spiritual experiment on yourself and on others. The New Testament calls us to something more stable: discernment in communion, correction in love, and leadership that watches over souls with fear of God.

Discussion Questions

1. Who currently has real permission to correct you about your tone, your content, or your behavior online? If the answer is "no one," what would it take to change that?

2. When you hear "submit to your leaders" (Hebrews 13:17), what emotions arise—comfort, suspicion, fear, anger? Why?

3. What does Galatians 2:11–14 teach you about confronting leaders when the Gospel is compromised? How might that apply online?

4. When controversies arise in the Church, do you tend to make them content quickly, or do you seek communal discernment and counsel first (Acts 15)?

5. If authority in your context has failed, what would a healthy path toward accountability and communion look like—without denial, and without cynicism?

Closing Prayer

Lord Jesus Christ, Shepherd of the Church, protect me from pride, isolation, and the illusion that I need no correction. Place me in healthy communion, under legitimate authority that watches over souls with reverence and love. Give me humility to submit where submission is faithful, courage to speak when truth requires it, and wisdom to seek discernment in community rather than in reaction. Heal the wounds caused by failed authority, protect the vulnerable, and purify your Church. Keep my online witness accountable, gentle, and true, so that I may serve others for your sake and help build up your Body in peace. Amen.

Chapter 13

Stewards of Mysteries: Reverence, Reserve, and "Pearls"

Online culture pressures Christians to speak as though everything must be immediately shareable. The platform loves exposure. It rewards disclosure, speed, and constant commentary. It assumes that the best response to any event is a post, and the best way to "teach" is to put everything on display, all at once, for anyone to consume. In that environment, Christianity can begin to feel like content—religious information delivered for maximum accessibility and engagement.

But the faith is not merely information. The faith is mystery.

"Mystery" in Christian language does not mean something vague or unknowable in principle. It means something real and revealed that remains greater than our comprehension. God is not an object we can fully grasp, and the Gospel is not a system we can flatten into slogans. Christian worship, sacramental life, and the deepest realities of the spiritual journey require reverence. And reverence often requires restraint.

This chapter argues that healthy digital mission must recover a virtue that online culture has nearly forgotten: **reverent reserve**. Not secrecy that hides wrongdoing, and not elitism that hoards knowledge, but the wise discipline of knowing when to speak, how much to reveal, and what should be shared only within appropriate pastoral and catechetical contexts. In other words: there are "pearls" that must be handled with care.

Stewards, not owners

Paul describes the basic identity of Christian ministers in a way that fits every Christian who speaks publicly about the faith: "This is how one should regard us, as servants of Christ and stewards of the mysteries of God. Moreover it is required of stewards that they be found trustworthy" (1 Corinthians 4:1–2, RSV). The word "steward" is crucial. A steward does not own what he carries. He is entrusted with something precious for the sake of others. His task is not to display himself, but to be faithful with what has been entrusted.

For the Christian influencer, this reframes everything. Your platform is not your possession. Your audience is not your property. And the mysteries you speak about are not raw material for engagement. You are handling holy realities—truths about God, salvation, sin, grace, worship, and the life of the Church. The question is not, "Will this perform?" The question is, "Is this trustworthy stewardship?"

Trustworthiness includes truthfulness, but it also includes reverence. It includes a sense of what is fitting, what is wise, what is pastorally appropriate, and what may harm rather than help when thrown into the open.

The platform temptation in this chapter: overexposure disguised as clarity

Many Christians sincerely want to be clear. Clarity is good. The Gospel should be proclaimed plainly. Christians should not hide behind fog or unnecessary obscurity. But online culture tempts us to confuse clarity with overexposure.

Overexposure happens when holy things are treated as ordinary, when sacred realities are reduced to content, when worship becomes entertainment, when spiritual counsel becomes spectacle, or when complex pastoral matters are discussed publicly in ways that increase scandal rather than encourage repentance. Overexposure can also happen when beginners are handed advanced material without formation, context, or protection. It is possible to be "technically correct" and still be spiritually reckless.

Clarity serves discipleship. Overexposure often serves engagement.

This is one reason the early Church practiced catechesis by stages and treated certain teachings with careful pastoral discretion. Not because the Church wanted to hide the Gospel, but because it wanted to form people gradually into the capacity to receive it. Not all truth is received the same way by an unformed heart. A person must learn reverence, humility, and repentance. They must be trained to approach holy things as holy. Without that formation, advanced teaching can become either misunderstood or mocked—or used as ammunition for ridicule.

"Do not give dogs what is holy"

Jesus speaks a sentence that modern online culture finds almost impossible to understand: "Do not give dogs what is holy; and do not throw your pearls before swine, lest they trample them under foot and turn to attack you" (Matthew 7:6, RSV). This verse is not permission to despise outsiders. It is a warning about spiritual prudence. Jesus assumes that some hearers will not receive holy things as holy. Some will treat them as objects for mockery. Some will use them as weapons. Some will trample what is sacred and then attack the one who offered it.

In other words, Jesus assumes that indiscriminate exposure can harm both the sacred thing and the speaker. The remedy is not cowardice. It is discernment. There is a difference between proclaiming the Gospel openly and exposing everything without regard for context.

The "pearls" Jesus refers to can include sacred practices, intimate pastoral realities, confessional matters, and deep mysteries of worship that require a formed heart. When these are thrown into the open without reverence, they are often not received as invitations to holiness. They are received as content for ridicule or as ammunition for controversy. The result is not evangelism but scandal.

A Christian creator must therefore ask: is what I am about to share holy in a way that requires a different context? Is my audience prepared? Is this the right moment? Is this the right medium? Or am I about to throw "pearls" into a space that will only trample them?

Treasure in earthen vessels

Paul adds another dimension that protects us from both arrogance and recklessness: "We have this treasure in earthen vessels, to show that the transcendent power belongs to God and not to us" (2 Corinthians 4:7, RSV). The treasure is real, and it is glorious. But it is carried by fragile people. That fragility matters online, because the temptation is to act as though we can manage sacred realities through sheer skill—through clever framing, perfect editing, or persuasive rhetoric. Paul says the opposite: God intentionally places treasure in fragile vessels so that the power is seen to be God's.

This also suggests why reverent reserve is necessary. Because we are earthen vessels, we are capable of mishandling the treasure. We can expose what should be protected. We can speak beyond our competence. We can turn what is sacred into spectacle. We can try to make mystery "manageable" for the sake of reach and end up trivializing what we claim to honor.

Humility means remembering that the mysteries of God exceed our control and our comprehension. Reverence means handling them with fear of God and love for souls.

Catechesis by stages: forming the capacity to receive

Digital ministry often throws every audience into one room: seekers, skeptics, new believers, mature disciples, the wounded, the hostile, the curious. Because the audience is mixed, the wise creator learns to teach in stages. This is not manipulation; it is pastoral care.

A beginner may need the simplest proclamation: Christ has died, Christ is risen, repent and believe. A seeker may need patient explanation and reassurance that questions are welcome. A baptized believer may need deeper formation in prayer, virtue, and worship. A person wrestling with sin may need private pastoral counsel, not public exposure. Mature disciples may be able to receive advanced theological reflection. But if you give advanced material to the unformed without context, it can confuse rather than build up.

This is why some content should be explicitly "introductory," some "intermediate," and some intended for those already committed to prayer and community. It is also why some matters should not be handled online at all. Certain spiritual struggles and confessional realities require privacy, trust, and embodied pastoral care.

Teaching by stages is one way to be a trustworthy steward.

When not to post

One of the most countercultural disciplines for Christian influencers is choosing not to post. The platform will tell you that silence is failure. Jesus tells you that reverence sometimes requires restraint.

Sometimes you should not post because you are angry and your speech will likely become contemptuous. Sometimes you should not post because you do not have verified facts. Sometimes you should not post because what you would share belongs to pastoral confidentiality or would expose someone else's vulnerability. Sometimes you should not post because your commentary would turn a sacred matter into a public spectacle. Sometimes you should not post because the medium itself is unsuitable for the depth required.

Silence can be an act of worship. It can also be an act of protection—protecting the holy thing, protecting the vulnerable, and protecting your own soul from being formed by constant reaction.

Scandal versus secrecy

At this point, the call to reserve can be misunderstood as a call to secrecy. They are not the same. Secrecy can be sinful when it hides abuse, enables wrongdoing, or protects reputations at the expense of victims. Reverent reserve, by contrast, is the wise guarding of what is holy and what is vulnerable.

The difference is the purpose. Secrecy protects power. Reserve protects holiness and persons. Secrecy avoids accountability. Reserve often seeks appropriate accountability in the right context. Secrecy hides sin. Reserve refuses to turn sin into spectacle.

Christian stewardship must never be used to excuse cover-ups. But Christian stewardship must also never be reduced to "expose everything to prove you're honest." The Gospel is not served by spiritual exhibitionism. It is served by truth and reverence together.

Trustworthy stewardship in the attention economy

To be "found trustworthy" (1 Corinthians 4:2) in the digital age is to resist the platform's demand for constant disclosure and constant commentary. It is to remember that you are not merely educating; you are shaping how people approach holy things. If you treat mysteries casually, your audience will learn casualness. If you treat them with reverence, your audience may learn reverence. If you turn sacred matters into entertainment, your audience will learn to consume religion rather than to worship God.

A Christian steward therefore aims not only at clarity, but at reverent clarity. Not only at accessibility, but at appropriate pacing. Not only at honesty, but at discretion. The goal is not to keep people out; the goal is to lead people in—gradually, faithfully, and safely—into the life of God.

We are servants, not owners. We are stewards, not entertainers. We carry treasure in earthen vessels. And the way we handle that treasure online can either invite people toward worship or train them toward triviality.

Discussion Questions

1. In your online work, where are you most tempted toward overexposure—sharing too much, too quickly, or in the wrong context? Why?

2. What "pearls" in the Christian faith require a different kind of reverence or a more careful setting than a public feed (Matthew 7:6)?

3. How can you teach in stages so that seekers and beginners are formed rather than overwhelmed?

4. When have you seen "clarity" become reckless exposure—creating scandal rather than discipleship? What was missing?

5. What might it look like for you to practice holy restraint—choosing not to post as an act of stewardship and worship?

Closing Prayer

Lord Jesus Christ, you have entrusted your Church with holy mysteries and made us stewards rather than owners. Give me reverence for what is sacred, wisdom for what is fitting, and courage to practice restraint when silence is more faithful than speech. Teach me not to throw pearls before swine, not out of contempt, but out of holy prudence and love for souls. Remind me that I carry treasure in an earthen vessel, and keep me trustworthy in all I share. May my words lead others into worship and communion with you, not into triviality or scandal, for you are Lord and all glory belongs to you. Amen.

Chapter 14

Enduring Criticism and Hardship: Prophets, Apostles, and Comment Sections

If you speak publicly about Christ, you will be criticized. Some criticism will be deserved. Some will be unfair. Some will be sharp but sincere. Some will be cruel and performative. Some will come from outsiders, and some will come from fellow Christians. Online platforms amplify all of it. They make misunderstanding travel fast, reward outrage, and turn misrepresentation into entertainment. And because the internet is always "on," criticism can feel inescapable—like you are living in a room where strangers can shout at you day and night.

This chapter is not meant to make you cynical, and it is not meant to romanticize suffering. It is meant to normalize a biblical fact: hardship is not an exception to Christian mission. It is often part of it. The prophets endured it. The apostles endured it. Jesus himself endured it. If you expect the comment section to be gentle simply because you are doing good work, you will be continually surprised and continually wounded. If you expect your motives to be understood, you will become easily discouraged. If you expect Christians to always support you, you will be unprepared for "friendly fire."

But if you learn to expect hardship in a sober, biblical way, you can endure it without losing your soul.

The platform temptation in this chapter: measuring calling by comfort

Online culture trains us to interpret discomfort as a sign we are doing something wrong. If you are criticized, you must have failed. If you are misunderstood, you must clarify immediately. If you are attacked, you must defend yourself at once. If your content creates conflict, you must either escalate the fight or retreat entirely.

The Gospel does not teach that. The Gospel teaches that faithfulness can be costly, and that righteousness does not guarantee comfort. If you tie your sense of calling to the amount of affirmation you receive, you will be unstable. You will become either addicted to praise or crushed by criticism. The platform will become your spiritual weather, and your soul will rise and fall with its temperature.

Scripture offers a different foundation: not comfort, but fidelity.

Paul's catalogue of suffering

Paul's description of hardship is bracing. He does not speak as a theorist of suffering, but as a man who has lived it: "In far greater labors, far more imprisonments, with countless beatings… five times I have received at the hands of the Jews the forty lashes less one… three times I have been beaten with rods… three times I have been shipwrecked… in toil and hardship, through many a sleepless night, in hunger and thirst… And, apart from other things, there is the daily pressure upon me of my anxiety for all the churches" (2 Corinthians 11:23–28, RSV).

It is impossible to read that paragraph and still imagine that faithful mission guarantees ease. Paul suffers physically, socially, emotionally, and spiritually. He is attacked from outside and pressured from within. He experiences danger, exhaustion, scarcity, and the constant burden of pastoral concern. Most modern Christian creators will never face anything like Paul's catalogue. But the passage still matters, because it redefines the meaning of hardship. It tells us that suffering is not necessarily a sign of failure. Sometimes it is simply the cost of love, the cost of truth, the cost of mission in a fallen world.

This passage also helps us name something many online ministers feel but rarely admit: "the daily pressure… anxiety for all the churches." Caring for people brings weight. And online ministry can magnify that weight because the needs seem endless and the crises seem constant. Paul's honesty gives permission to be honest. Burden is not always sin. Sometimes it is the mark of a heart that loves.

Yet Paul's catalogue also implies a warning: no human being can carry everything. If you try to carry the whole internet, you will break. Part of enduring hardship is learning what is yours to carry and what must be handed back to God.

Jeremiah's conflicted fire

The prophets show another side of hardship: the internal struggle of being called to speak when speech is costly. Jeremiah confesses something almost shocking in its intensity. He feels deceived and mocked, he becomes "a laughingstock," and he tries to stop speaking. But he discovers he cannot: "If I say, 'I will not mention him, or speak any more in his name,' there is in my heart as it were a burning fire shut up in my bones, and I am weary with holding it in, and I cannot" (Jeremiah 20:7–9, RSV).

This is what calling can feel like: not constant confidence, but compelled fidelity. Jeremiah does not always feel strong. He feels pressure, grief, and fatigue. He feels misunderstood. He feels mocked. Yet the word of God is like fire in his bones. He cannot abandon it.

Online ministry can produce a smaller version of this tension. After enough slander, misrepresentation, and hostility, you may want to go silent permanently. Sometimes silence is needed, for rest and healing. But Jeremiah reminds us that there can also be a holy persistence—an endurance that is not fueled by stubbornness, but by the sense that God has placed something in you that must be spoken, even if it costs you.

Jeremiah also teaches another crucial truth: endurance does not require you to pretend everything is fine. His prayer is honest. If prophets can speak honestly to God about discouragement, you can too.

Jesus' beatitude for the criticized

Jesus speaks directly to the experience of being attacked for righteousness: "Blessed are you when men revile you and persecute you and utter all kinds of evil against you falsely on my account. Rejoice and be glad, for your reward is great in heaven" (Matthew 5:11–12, RSV). The key word is "falsely." Jesus assumes misrepresentation. He assumes slander. He assumes malicious speech. And he places that experience in the context of union with him—"on my account."

This beatitude is not an invitation to seek persecution or to interpret every criticism as righteousness. Some criticism is needed correction. But when you are genuinely slandered for Christ's sake, Jesus tells you that you are not abandoned. You are sharing in a pattern that belongs to the prophets: "so persecuted they the prophets who were before you" (Matthew 5:12).

This is one of the deepest comforts available to Christian creators: you are not alone in being misunderstood. The saints have walked this path. The prophets have walked this path. Christ himself has walked this path.

Friendly fire and the pain of intra-Christian conflict

Some of the hardest criticism will come from fellow Christians. Sometimes it will be charitable and helpful. Sometimes it will be tribal. Sometimes it will be driven by fear, envy, or factional loyalty rather than by love of truth. Intra-Christian conflict can feel especially painful because you expect family to be different from strangers.

Paul's catalogue in 2 Corinthians includes "anxiety for all the churches," and that anxiety often comes precisely because communities are messy, leaders are imperfect, and Christians can wound each other. If you are not prepared for this, you may either become bitter or withdraw into a private spirituality that abandons mission.

The remedy is not to stop caring. The remedy is to endure with wisdom. That means distinguishing between correction you should receive and hostility you should not internalize. It means learning to say, "I will listen carefully," without saying, "I will let this define me." And it means remembering that unity is not the same as appeasement. You can pursue peace without surrendering truth.

Safeguarding mental health without abandoning mission

Endurance is not the same as self-destruction. Some Christians treat burnout as a badge of faithfulness. That is not biblical. Jesus himself withdrew to pray. He rested. He stepped away from crowds. Paul had companions. The Church is not served by creators who grind themselves into despair.

Safeguarding mental health begins with accepting limits. You cannot read every comment. You cannot respond to every accusation. You cannot correct every misunderstanding. You cannot carry every crisis. The platform will constantly suggest otherwise, because it profits from your constant engagement. But your mind is not a machine, and your soul is not an unlimited resource. If you want to endure, you must practice restraint.

It is also wise to develop a sober approach to criticism. Not all criticism deserves attention. Some is noise. Some is projection. Some is trolling. Some is sincere but uninformed. Some is accurate and necessary. Endurance requires discernment: the ability to receive what is true, reject what is malicious, and let God be your judge.

Practically, this can include limiting how often you check comments, setting boundaries around DMs, delegating moderation if possible, and taking regular breaks. It can include intentionally cultivating offline relationships and embodied community so that your sense of reality is not shaped solely by online reactions. It can include spiritual direction or therapy when the weight becomes too heavy. Seeking help is not a lack of faith. It is often an act of humility.

The goal is not to harden your heart. The goal is to protect your heart so that it can remain tender without becoming fragile.

Endurance without defensiveness

One of the easiest ways criticism destroys ministry is by making the creator defensive. Defensiveness can become a constant posture: always explaining, always justifying, always reacting. This is exhausting, and it often makes your speech less truthful because it is shaped by fear.

A more stable posture is to remember Romans 14: we will all stand before God. The crowd is not your judge. The comment section is not your judge. God is your judge. That does not mean you ignore correction, but it means you do not live by public verdicts. You can listen carefully, repent when necessary, clarify when helpful, and then return to faithfulness without living in constant defense.

Jeremiah's fire and Paul's endurance suggest that mission is sustained not by constant emotional strength but by deep spiritual rootedness. And Jesus' beatitude suggests that false accusations, while painful, are not meaningless. They can become occasions for deeper humility and deeper union with Christ.

Enduring hardship online does not mean you never feel hurt. It means you learn to suffer in a way that does not make you bitter, cruel, or despairing. It means you learn to keep loving, keep praying, keep telling the truth, and keep protecting your soul. The mission continues, not because the comment section becomes kind, but because Christ remains Lord.

Discussion Questions

1. When criticism comes, what is your default response: immediate defense, withdrawal, anger, despair, or prayerful discernment? Why?

2. How can Paul's catalogue of sufferings (2 Corinthians 11:23–28) reframe the way you interpret hardship in ministry—without romanticizing it?

3. In what ways do you feel Jeremiah's "fire in the bones" (Jeremiah 20:9)? In what ways do you feel weary and tempted to silence?

4. What boundaries would help protect your mental and spiritual health (comment limits, scheduled breaks, moderation, accountability) without abandoning your mission?

5. How do you distinguish between criticism you should receive as correction and slander you should release to God (Matthew 5:11–12)?

Closing Prayer

Lord Jesus Christ, you were reviled and misunderstood, yet you did not abandon your mission. Give me endurance when criticism comes, wisdom to discern what is true, and humility to repent where I am wrong. Protect me from bitterness, from defensiveness, and from the temptation to measure calling by comfort. When I am mocked or misrepresented, remind me that I stand before your judgment seat, not the crowd's. When I am weary, renew me. When the fire of calling burns, keep it holy and humble. Grant me the grace to endure hardship with joy in you, and to safeguard my mind and heart so that I may continue to serve faithfully. Amen.

Chapter 15

Vocation or Job? Money, Patronage, and the Burden on the Church

Sooner or later, anyone doing Christian work online runs into the money question. It may arrive gently—someone asks how to support your work. Or it may arrive suddenly—platform monetization opens, a sponsor offers a contract, or a donor proposes monthly funding. At first, it can feel like a simple practical matter: equipment costs money, time costs money, and good resources often require sustained labor.

But Scripture refuses to treat money as a merely practical topic. Money touches the heart. It exposes motives. It can strengthen ministry—or quietly poison it. And in online spaces, the pressure is intense because platforms blur boundaries between ministry, brand, and business. A creator can begin as an evangelist and, without noticing, become a religious entrepreneur whose livelihood depends on constant engagement, constant controversy, and constant fundraising.

This chapter is not an argument that Christian creators must never be paid. The New Testament does not teach that. It is an argument that Christian creators must treat money with fear of God, transparent integrity, and a sober awareness of how easily "support" can turn into manipulation and how easily "ministry" can turn into a product.

Paul's paradox: rights, restraint, and the Gospel offered freely

Paul addresses financial support with unusual clarity and personal vulnerability in 1 Corinthians 9. He argues that ministers of the Gospel have real rights—real permission to receive support. Yet he also describes a surprising choice: he often refuses to make use of those rights. "Nevertheless, we have not made use of this right, but we endure anything rather than put an obstacle in the way of the gospel of Christ" (1 Corinthians 9:12, RSV).

That sentence reveals a basic ethical principle for all Christian influence: even if something is permitted, it may not be wise. Paul's question is not, "Can I?" but "Will this hinder the Gospel?" He does not want money to become an obstacle—either by burdening new believers, confusing outsiders, or giving critics an easy reason to dismiss the message as a hustle.

He goes further. He insists that his work is not a performance for profit: "What then is my reward? Just this: that in my preaching I may make the gospel free of charge, not making full use of my right in the gospel" (1 Corinthians 9:18, RSV). Paul is protecting something sacred: the perception and reality that the Gospel itself is not being sold. He is guarding the "free" character of grace. He is also guarding his own heart. Money can attach itself to ministry like a vine, and soon the ministry cannot move without money pulling on it.

Online ministry must learn Paul's paradox. There may be legitimate reasons to receive support, and there may also be legitimate reasons to refuse certain forms of support. The question is not only what funds your work; the question is what your funding does to your soul, your message, and your audience.

The platform temptation in this chapter: turning disciples into customers

The internet is built to monetize attention. When Christian creators monetize, they step onto a moving walkway that naturally carries them toward a specific logic: keep people watching, keep them emotionally engaged, keep them dependent, and keep them paying.

That logic can quietly reshape content. Controversy becomes profitable because outrage drives views. Fear becomes profitable because fear drives loyalty. Constant crisis becomes profitable because crisis keeps donors "activated." Even if the creator does not consciously choose these things, the incentives are there, and incentives form habits.

The deeper danger is spiritual: people begin to relate to the creator not primarily as a fellow disciple but as a provider. The creator becomes a vendor of spiritual goods. The audience becomes a customer base. And Christian giving—meant to be joyful and voluntary—can become guilt-driven patronage, sustained by emotional pressure rather than by discernment.

This is one reason money issues are never "just logistics." They directly affect discipleship.

"Those who desire to be rich…": the spiritual risk of greed

Paul warns Timothy with language that is blunt precisely because the danger is subtle: "Those who desire to be rich fall into temptation, into a snare… For the love of money is the root of all evils" (1 Timothy 6:9–10, RSV). Notice that he targets not money itself, but desire—an inward orientation that makes wealth the goal. The danger is not limited to millionaires. A person can "desire to be rich" at any scale, and that desire can turn ministry into a ladder of ambition.

For the Christian influencer, this warning lands in a particular way. Platforms constantly display the "successful" creator: the polished studio, the sponsorships, the lifestyle, the steady income. It is easy to begin comparing. It is easy to begin justifying compromises because "this is how the work can grow." And it is easy, very easy, to baptize ambition as mission.

Paul calls it a snare because it captures you gradually. You do not wake up one morning deciding to manipulate donors. You simply begin to need a certain level of income, and then you begin to fear losing it, and then you begin to shape content to protect it. The work becomes less about obedience and more about maintenance. The ministry becomes a machine that must be fed.

The love of money is not only the craving for luxury. It is the refusal to be free.

Integrity and generosity: what 2 Corinthians 8–9 teaches creators

In 2 Corinthians 8–9, Paul addresses a collection for needy believers and emphasizes themes that should shape all Christian fundraising: integrity, transparency, generosity, and freedom. He insists that giving must not be coerced. "Each one must do as he has made up his mind, not reluctantly or under compulsion, for God loves a cheerful giver" (2 Corinthians 9:7, RSV). That sentence is a direct rebuke to manipulative fundraising tactics. If your giving appeals depend on guilt, fear, shame, or spiritual threats, you are no longer practicing Christian stewardship. You are practicing coercion.

Paul also cares about accountability. He wants the collection handled in a way that prevents scandal and protects trust. The point is not merely "raise money for a good cause," but "do it in a way that honors God and avoids reproach." For digital ministries, this translates into a sober commitment to honesty: being clear about what funds are for, refusing vague emotional appeals that conceal real financial needs, and establishing safeguards so that money does not become a private slush fund.

2 Corinthians 8–9 also reframes giving as participation in grace. Generosity is not buying influence with God or with the minister. It is sharing in God's own generosity. When creators speak about support, they must guard that theological truth. Donation is not payment for access. It is not a fee for spiritual belonging. It is a voluntary act of love.

Vocation or job: discerning what kind of work this is

For some, digital mission will remain a vocation alongside ordinary work. For others, it may become a full-time labor supported by donors, patrons, or an institution. Scripture allows for both, but it does not treat them as spiritually identical.

If your online ministry becomes a job, then you face a new set of temptations. You may begin to feel you must speak constantly because silence feels like not "earning" your support. You may begin to treat your audience as a payroll. You may begin to avoid hard truths because they might cost subscribers. Or you may begin to chase controversy because it increases revenue. The issue is not simply ethics; it is formation. Your livelihood can begin to form your message.

Paul's example helps here because he shows that sometimes restraint is evangelistically strategic. "We endure anything rather than put an obstacle in the way of the gospel" (1 Corinthians 9:12). There may be seasons when refusing monetization protects your witness. There may be seasons when receiving support is legitimate, but only if you can do so without placing a burden on the Church, without manipulating donors, and without confusing the Gospel with a product.

A crucial question, then, is whether you can remain faithful when money is at stake. Can you speak truth even if it costs you subscribers? Can you admit error even if it weakens your "brand"? Can you slow down, rest, or step away even if it reduces income? If not, you are not free—and if you are not free, you are vulnerable to being controlled by the very system you are trying to use for mission.

Practical integrity: keeping ministry, brand, and business distinct

In the attention economy, the simplest way to guard your soul is to make your financial practices boringly transparent and structurally accountable. Not to perform virtue, but to remove opportunities for self-deception.

Integrity means being honest about what you are doing. If you are running a business that sells products, say so. If you are receiving donations for ministry work, say what that work is. If you are receiving sponsorships, disclose them clearly and refuse sponsors that distort your message. If donors are funding your time, be honest about how that affects your schedule and priorities.

Integrity also means refusing donor manipulation. You should never imply that giving makes someone spiritually superior, or that disagreement is disloyalty because "we need to keep the lights on." You should never treat donors as leverage in church disputes or theological arguments. And you should be cautious about creating environments where followers feel obligated to support you as proof of faithfulness.

Just as importantly, integrity requires boundaries. Some supporters will want more access, more intimacy, more private counsel, more influence over your content, more emotional dependence. Money can intensify parasocial attachment, and attachment can become a form of spiritual bondage for both donor and creator. Christian stewardship must protect people from that. It must direct them back toward Christ and the local Church, not deeper into dependence on a creator.

In all of this, the guiding principle is the same: the Gospel is not for sale. Grace is not a product. And Christian giving must remain free—free from compulsion, free from manipulation, and free from the worship of money.

Paul's voice remains steady across these passages. He recognizes legitimate rights, but he is willing to surrender them for the sake of the Gospel. He warns against the love of money because it ruins souls. And he insists that generosity must be handled with integrity and joy, not compulsion. That is the path forward for Christian online mission in a monetized world: freedom, truthfulness, and trustworthiness.

Discussion Questions

1. In your heart, do you want online ministry to be primarily a vocation or a job? What fears or desires are shaping that answer?

2. How might monetization change what you post, how often you post, and what you avoid? Are you willing to accept those pressures?

3. Have you ever felt manipulated by religious fundraising online? What made it feel coercive rather than joyful (2 Corinthians 9:7)?

4. What boundaries would protect you and your audience from turning discipleship into a customer relationship?

5. If receiving support could "put an obstacle in the way of the gospel" (1 Corinthians 9:12), what would faithful restraint look like in your case?

Closing Prayer

Lord Jesus Christ, you have given the Gospel freely, and you call your servants to be trustworthy stewards. Deliver me from greed, from the love of money, and from every temptation to turn ministry into a brand or disciples into customers. Give me wisdom to discern when to accept support and when to refuse it for the sake of the Gospel. Teach me integrity in all financial matters, gentleness and clarity in every appeal, and gratitude for every gift offered freely. Make my heart content in you, my hands clean in stewardship, and my work a witness that points beyond money to your grace. Amen.

Chapter 16

Authentic Faith: Light in the World, Not Merely Winning Arguments

Online Christian spaces can easily become a world made of words. There are endless arguments to answer, endless claims to correct, endless controversies to comment on. A person can spend hours each day "defending the faith" and yet never forgive an enemy, never serve a neighbor, never pray with attention, never visit the sick, never reconcile with family, never worship with a community, never practice generosity in secret. In other words, a person can sound Christian online while slowly becoming less Christian in real life.

This is not because apologetics and teaching are bad. They are often necessary. But Scripture insists that the truth of Christian witness is not finally proven by rhetorical victories. It is proven by holiness, love, and obedience—by a life that shines.

Jesus does not say, "You are the winners of arguments." He says, "You are the light of the world" (Matthew 5:14, RSV). Light is not noise. Light is not performance. Light is a lived reality that reveals what is good and true by simply being present. When Christians live authentically, their lives become a kind of testimony that words alone cannot replace.

The platform temptation in this chapter: substituting commentary for discipleship

Platforms encourage Christianity-as-commentary. They reward the creator who always has a take, always has an explanation, always has an opponent, always has a rebuttal. Over time, Christian identity can drift into a posture of analysis rather than obedience. The faith becomes something we talk about rather than something we practice.

This temptation is especially strong for those who are intellectually gifted. It is possible to love theology and yet avoid conversion. It is possible to become skillful at describing virtues and yet resist living them. And because online life is so word-driven, it can give the illusion of spiritual productivity even when the heart is unchanged.

Scripture exposes this illusion. The Christian is not called merely to hear truth, but to do it.

"You are the light of the world"

Jesus places public witness in the context of embodied life: "You are the light of the world. A city set on a hill cannot be hid... Let your light so shine before men, that they may see your good works and give glory to your Father who is in heaven" (Matthew 5:14–16, RSV). Notice what Jesus emphasizes. He does not say, "Let your light shine so they may see your correct arguments." He says, "that they may see your good works."

Good works do not earn salvation. They reveal it. They are not the cause of grace, but the fruit of grace. And Jesus says those works have a missionary effect: they lead others to glorify the Father. A life shaped by mercy, humility, fidelity, courage, and service can make the Gospel plausible in a way that arguments cannot.

Online apologetics may remove obstacles. It may answer questions. It may clarify misunderstandings. But it cannot replace a life of goodness. If your content is brilliant but your character is bitter, you will eventually undermine your own witness. If your arguments are sharp but your relationships are broken, your light will flicker. If you "win" online but do not love your neighbor, you are not shining; you are performing.

"Be doers of the word"

James confronts the heart of the problem with unforgettable directness: "Be doers of the word, and not hearers only, deceiving yourselves" (James 1:22, RSV). The phrase "deceiving yourselves" is the key. James assumes that religious people can deceive themselves by mistaking exposure to truth for obedience to truth. Hearing becomes a substitute for doing. In the digital world, watching becomes a substitute for living. Consuming Christian content becomes a substitute for prayer, repentance, and service.

James is not anti-intellectual. He is anti-self-deception. He is warning that Christianity can become a form of spiritual entertainment—a thing we "follow" rather than a path we walk. This is why the internet can be spiritually dangerous: it makes it easy to feel involved without being transformed.

A Christian creator must therefore ask a hard question: is my online work helping people do the word, or merely helping them feel informed? And even more personally: is my online work helping me do the word, or merely helping me feel righteous?

"By this all men will know..."

Jesus gives the simplest test of Christian credibility: "By this all men will know that you are my disciples, if you have love for one another" (John 13:35, RSV). Notice: the identifying mark is not brilliance, not controversy, not cultural influence, not doctrinal combativeness. It is love.

Love is not vague sentiment. Love is patience, kindness, truthfulness, and sacrifice. Love is forgiveness. Love is refusing contempt. Love is bearing burdens. Love is serving in hidden ways. Love is staying faithful in community when community is inconvenient.

This is why embodied Christianity matters so much. Love is not learned primarily through content. Love is learned through relationships—through the slow school of life together, where we must practice humility, confession, reconciliation, and mutual service. Online life can support that, but it cannot replace it. The Christian who is not rooted in actual community is at risk of becoming a kind of disembodied thinker who speaks about love while rarely practicing it.

Embodied Christianity: community, worship, service, and the "ordinary" life

The Gospel does not make us floating spiritual minds. It calls us into a Body. It calls us into worship. It calls us into tangible acts of mercy. For many Christians, it also includes sacramental life—baptism, Eucharist, confession, and the rhythms of prayer and liturgy—as the means by which Christ forms his people. Even in traditions that speak differently about sacraments, the principle remains: the faith is embodied, communal, and practiced.

This is crucial for Christian influencers because platforms can create a false sense of "church." A creator's community can begin to function like a congregation without the protections and responsibilities of a congregation. People confess in DMs. They seek spiritual counsel from a stranger. They form identity around online belonging. Meanwhile, the ordinary local church—imperfect, slow, unglamorous—can be neglected.

But disciples are formed in the ordinary. They are formed by worship with real people, by serving in quiet ways, by forgiving those who annoy you, by staying faithful when the music is bad and the sermon is boring, by showing up when no one is watching. Online audiences can affirm you; local community can sanctify you.

A mature Christian creator learns to direct people away from dependence on the platform and toward the embodied practices of faith: prayer, Scripture, worship, service, reconciliation, and community. The goal is not to make people loyal to your channel. The goal is to help them become disciples who can live the Gospel on Tuesday morning when no one is filming.

Apologetics versus holiness: what each can and cannot do

Apologetics is valuable. It can clarify misconceptions, answer objections, and remove intellectual barriers that keep people from taking Christ seriously. But apologetics cannot, by itself, make someone holy. It cannot, by itself, teach someone to forgive. It cannot, by itself, form someone into patience. It cannot, by itself, produce love.

Holiness is formed through grace received and practiced: through prayer, repentance, worship, obedience, and the life of the Church. Holiness is the slow transformation of a person into the likeness of Christ. This is why a creator who wants to do digital mission must keep asking: does my content serve holiness? Does it lead people toward obedience, love, and community? Or does it simply keep them in a cycle of watching, debating, and consuming?

The same question must be asked inwardly. Does your content calendar leave space for your soul? Do you have time for prayer that is not "research"? Do you serve anyone who cannot benefit your platform? Do you have relationships where you are not the teacher, not the leader, not the voice—just a fellow Christian?

If not, the platform may be forming you more than Christ is.

Letting your life carry the message

Jesus says, "Let your light so shine... that they may see your good works" (Matthew 5:16). The word "see" matters. The Gospel is heard, but it is also seen. Many people come to faith not because they lost an argument, but because they witnessed a life that was different—humble, patient, joyful, generous, courageous, and loving in ways that did not make sense without God.

For online missionaries, this means your credibility will eventually depend on what you embody. Your audience may not see your entire life, and they should not. But they will see your tone, your patience, your honesty, your willingness to repent, your refusal to dehumanize, your commitment to the local church, and your prioritizing of love over victory. Those things are visible. And they either shine or they do not.

Authentic faith is therefore not anti-intellectual. It is a reminder of order. Arguments serve discipleship; they do not replace it. Online work can assist mission; it cannot replace embodied life. Knowledge matters; love reveals. The call is not merely to win, but to shine.

Discussion Questions

1. Do you spend more time consuming or creating Christian content than praying, serving, and practicing the faith in embodied ways? What does that reveal?

2. How might "good works" (Matthew 5:16) look in your actual daily life—especially in hidden ways no audience will see?

3. In what ways might you be deceiving yourself by being a "hearer" (or "watcher") rather than a doer (James 1:22)?

4. Are you rooted in a local Christian community where you are known and accountable? If not, what step could you take toward that?

5. If someone judged your discipleship by John 13:35, would love be the most obvious feature of your life and speech?

Closing Prayer

Lord Jesus Christ, Light of the world, forgive me for the times I have mistaken words for obedience and arguments for holiness. Make me a doer of your word and not a hearer only. Teach me to let my light shine through good works, humble service, and love for your people, so that others may give glory to the Father. Root me in prayer, worship, and embodied community, and keep my online witness from becoming a substitute for communion with you. Form me into love, that all may know I am your disciple. Amen.

Chapter 17

No Christianity Based on Hate: Creation, Neighbor, and the Image of God

The internet is excellent at manufacturing enemies. It gathers people into tribes, rewards outrage, and trains communities to bond through shared contempt. In religious spaces, this can look like "discernment" that is really mockery, or "courage" that is really cruelty, or "defending the faith" that is really the pleasure of having targets. Over time, a community can begin to feel spiritually energized precisely because it is angry—because it has villains, scandals, and enemies to denounce.

But there is no Christianity based on hate.

This is not a sentimental slogan. It is a theological claim rooted in creation, in the commandments, and in the Gospel. You cannot love God while training your heart to despise those made in God's image. You cannot proclaim Christ while cultivating contempt as a habit. You cannot speak "truth" in a way that erodes human dignity and still claim to be witnessing faithfully.

Christians will face hard moral questions. The world will demand clarity about sin, justice, sexuality, power, and public life. But Scripture insists that even when we must speak hard truths, we must speak them in a way that protects the person—because the person is not disposable. The person is someone for whom Christ died.

The platform temptation in this chapter: contempt-based "community"

Some online communities are held together primarily by shared contempt. They may call it "being awake," "being faithful," "being uncompromising," or "seeing through the lies." But the glue is often hatred: hatred for a class of people, a political group, another denomination, a social movement, or a stigmatized minority. The community grows because contempt is intoxicating. It makes people feel pure, superior, and safe.

This is spiritually deadly. It deforms the heart. It trains people to enjoy cruelty. It makes repentance harder. And it makes the Gospel unbelievable to outsiders, who see not good news but a religious permission-slip for hostility.

If a Christian creator wants to do online mission faithfully, they must refuse to build or feed contempt-based communities. Even when addressing genuine error or sin, the Christian must never treat a person or group as subhuman, disposable, or unworthy of love.

The image of God is the foundation of human dignity

Scripture's first word about human worth is not achievement, intelligence, usefulness, or moral purity. It is creation: "So God created man in his own image, in the image of God he created him; male and female he created them" (Genesis 1:27, RSV). Human dignity is not earned. It is bestowed. Every person bears the image of God. That image may be wounded by sin, obscured by ignorance, or twisted by evil, but it is still real.

This has immediate consequences for Christian speech online. If the person you are addressing bears God's image, then mockery becomes a kind of sacrilege. Dehumanizing language becomes a form of spiritual vandalism. And communities built on contempt become anti-creational: they treat God's handiwork as disposable.

This does not mean Christians pretend moral differences do not matter. It means moral discourse must always occur on the foundation of dignity. Even when we must say "this is wrong," we must never imply "you are worthless." Even when we must name sin, we must not deny the person's humanity.

The image of God is why Christians defend the vulnerable, advocate for justice, resist racism and cruelty, oppose abuse, and insist that no one is "outside" the reach of God's mercy. It is also why Christians must discipline their own tongues. The person behind the screen is not a target. They are an icon of God's image—whether they act like it or not.

You cannot love God while hating your brother

John's language is uncompromising: "If any one says, 'I love God,' and hates his brother, he is a liar" (1 John 4:20, RSV). That is a hard sentence, and it is meant to be. John does not allow a separation between vertical devotion and horizontal hatred. Love of God and love of neighbor are intertwined. If you claim to love the God you cannot see while despising the human you can see, your claim is false.

John continues: "And this commandment we have from him, that he who loves God should love his brother also" (1 John 4:21, RSV). This is not an optional spiritual "extra." It is a commandment. And because it is a commandment, it applies not only to how we feel but to how we act and speak. If your online presence trains you toward hatred, it is training you away from God.

In the attention economy, this becomes a diagnostic test. If your content depends on stirring hatred, you are not doing Christian mission. If your audience is becoming more contemptuous over time, something is wrong—not merely in strategy, but in spirit.

The neighbor is not your tribe: the Good Samaritan

When asked, "Who is my neighbor?" Jesus answers with a story that dismantles tribal definitions of love: the parable of the Good Samaritan (Luke 10:25–37). A man is beaten and left for dead. A priest passes by. A Levite passes by. A Samaritan—an outsider, a member of a despised group—stops, has compassion, binds wounds, and pays for care.

Jesus' point is not subtle. Neighbor-love is not limited to people like you. It crosses boundaries of tribe, purity, and identity. And neighbor-love is not merely an attitude. It is action: stopping, tending wounds, bearing cost, and refusing to leave someone suffering on the roadside.

Online, we often face "neighbors" we would never choose: opponents, critics, the confused, the hostile, the wounded, the morally compromised. The temptation is to pass by on the other side—or worse, to become part of the crowd that throws stones at the wounded man. Jesus' parable calls Christians to a different instinct: compassion that sees a human being before it sees a category.

This is crucial for how Christians speak about hard moral issues. If you speak about sexuality, identity, politics, or sin in a way that ignores real wounds and real vulnerability, you may be "correct" in some abstract sense and still be unfaithful in love. The Samaritan sees the person. The Christian must learn to do the same.

Speaking truth on hard moral issues while protecting the person

At this point, a Christian might ask: how do we avoid hate without surrendering truth? The answer is not to become vague. The answer is to become disciplined in love.

Protecting the person while addressing moral issues involves several habits. It begins with refusing slurs, mockery, and dismissive labels. Even when a culture uses harsh terms, the Christian must speak as a disciple of Christ. If the only way you can address an issue is by ridiculing people, then you are not ready to address it.

It also involves distinguishing persons from ideologies and choices. You may need to critique an idea or a practice. But you must never treat the person as disposable. People are not arguments. They are not symbols. They are not threats to be eliminated. They are neighbors to be loved. Love does not require affirming every choice; it requires willing the good of the other, which includes truth, mercy, and hope.

Speaking truth faithfully also requires refusing to build communities around disgust. Some online ministries attract audiences primarily because they provide permission to hate. That is a spiritual trap. If your "community" grows because it gives people a sense of moral superiority and an enemy to despise, you are not forming disciples. You are forming a faction.

Finally, protecting the person requires remembering the Gospel's posture: Jesus does not merely confront sin; he offers redemption. Christian speech that talks about sin without offering grace becomes crushing. Christian speech that offers grace without truth becomes sentimental. The Gospel holds both together: "neither do I condemn you... go, and do not sin again" (cf. John 8:11). The Christian must learn to speak with that same seriousness and mercy.

Refusing contempt as a spiritual discipline

Because the internet rewards contempt, refusing it must become a discipline rather than a mood. You will not always feel charitable. You will be provoked. You will be misunderstood. You will see genuine evil. In those moments, refusing contempt does not mean refusing truth; it means refusing dehumanization.

This discipline can look like slowing down, praying before responding, asking what your words will do to the vulnerable, and remembering that the image of God is present even in the person who irritates you. It can look like choosing to speak in ways that a real neighbor could hear—imagining the person across the table rather than behind the screen. It can also look like leaving spaces that feed hatred, even if those spaces are "Christian" in name. A community that forms you into contempt is not a healthy community, no matter what doctrines it claims.

The Christian creator must therefore choose what kind of spirit will govern their ministry. The spirit of hate is loud and profitable. The spirit of Christ is often quieter, slower, and costly. But it is the only spirit that can truly evangelize.

Genesis tells you who people are: bearers of God's image. John tells you what love of God requires: love of neighbor. Jesus tells you who your neighbor is: the one in front of you, even if he is an enemy, even if he is wounded, even if he is "other." From these truths comes a simple conclusion: there is no Christianity based on hate.

Discussion Questions

1. Have you ever found yourself drawn to a "Christian" community mainly because it gave you permission to despise others? What did it do to your heart over time?

2. How does Genesis 1:27 reshape the way you should speak about people you strongly disagree with?

3. When you discuss hard moral issues online, do your words protect the dignity of persons, or do they treat people as symbols and targets?

4. In the Good Samaritan story (Luke 10:25–37), what would "crossing the road" look like in digital life—compassionate action rather than commentary?

5. If 1 John 4:20–21 were used as a mirror for your online presence, what would it reveal about love, hatred, and the habits your content is forming?

Closing Prayer

God of all creation, you have made every person in your image and called us to love our neighbor as ourselves. Forgive me for the ways I have allowed contempt, mockery, or hatred to enter my speech and harden my heart. Deliver me from building or joining communities formed by hatred. Give me courage to speak truthfully, wisdom to speak carefully, and love that protects the dignity of every person even when I must address hard moral realities. Teach me to see my neighbor, to have compassion, and to act in mercy like the Good Samaritan. Make my witness a light that reflects your love, through Jesus Christ our Lord. Amen.

Chapter 18

The Online Church and the Parish Church: Why the Digital World Can Mislead

Many people first encounter Christianity—or a particular tradition—through the internet. They watch articulate apologists, follow clergy and theologians, listen to podcasts, and join online communities that speak fluently about doctrine, history, liturgy, and the spiritual life. For some, this becomes the doorway to conversion or renewal. That is a genuine gift. The internet can offer access to beauty, learning, and encouragement that a person's local situation may not provide.

But this gift carries a quiet danger: **the online Christian world often does not resemble the real world of ordinary parishes and congregations.** If we do not name this honestly, people can be set up for disappointment, disillusionment, or even cynicism. They convert to a tradition they encountered online—and then discover that the lived experience in the average parish does not match the digital showcase.

This chapter offered as a realism check and a pastoral guide. It aims to protect converts, seekers, and returning believers from false expectations, and to help online evangelists speak about the Church more truthfully.

1) Why online Christianity can feel "more real" than the parish

The internet selects for intensity. People who spend their time producing theological content are usually the highly motivated: the readers, the debaters, the enthusiasts, the ones who care enough to study, argue, and explain. They often represent the most articulate and most engaged layer of a tradition. Their work can be excellent—sometimes even extraordinary. But the very excellence can create an illusion: it can make that layer feel like "the norm."

Parish life, by contrast, is not selected for intensity. The average parish is a mixture of every kind of person: the devout and the distracted, the deeply formed and the barely catechized, the weekly worshipper and the occasional attender, the enthusiastic volunteer and the exhausted parent just trying to survive the week. In most communities, people are not thinking about theology constantly. They are thinking about work, childcare, medical bills, loneliness, grief, addiction, and the daily grind of life.

Online Christianity is often a world of **arguments and ideals**. Parish Christianity is often a world of **habits and survival**. Both are real, but they are not the same, and confusing them leads to disillusionment.

2) The "apologist gap": catechesis online vs catechesis in the pew

Consider one clear example: Roman Catholic apologetics online compared to the average Catholic in a typical parish. Online, one can find Catholics with sharp command of Scripture, councils, papal documents, patristics, Thomistic categories, liturgical history, and intricate debates with Protestants, Orthodox, atheists, or modern moral philosophies. This can give the impression that "Catholics" generally know their tradition at that level.

Then a person visits an ordinary parish and discovers a different reality. Many Catholics have limited catechesis. Some are deeply faithful but not articulate. Some are cultural Catholics with minimal formation. Some have serious misunderstandings of basic doctrines. Some are sincere but poorly taught. Some are carrying wounds from past experiences. Parish RCIA or adult formation might be excellent—or it might be thin, inconsistent, or dependent on volunteers with uneven preparation.

This is not unique to Catholicism. It happens across traditions: online Orthodox spaces can feel intensely theological and liturgically serious compared to many local communities; online Evangelical spaces can feel Scripture-saturated and mission-driven compared to congregations where many are biblically under-formed; online "high church" Anglican spaces can feel intellectually and aesthetically rich compared to ordinary parish realities. The pattern is consistent:

- **Online:** concentrated excellence, specialization, strong identity, high engagement
- **Parish:** mixed formation, uneven catechesis, competing priorities, ordinary life

The internet can easily present the best "argument" version of a tradition. The parish often reveals the "human" version: sincere people who are partly formed, partly confused, partly faithful, and still growing.

3) Why this gap creates disappointment (and why it shouldn't)

When someone converts or returns to faith based on an online impression, they may carry expectations like these:

- "People will talk about theology like this all the time."
- "The parish will have deep formation and strong community."
- "The liturgy will be reverent and consistent everywhere."

- "Most people will share my level of interest and seriousness."
- "I will quickly find my 'tribe' and feel at home."

Sometimes those expectations are met. Often they are not. And when they are not met, a person may conclude that the tradition itself is hollow or fraudulent. But that conclusion does not follow. The more accurate conclusion is simpler: **the Church is a hospital, not a seminar.** The parish is where ordinary Christians stumble toward holiness together, often slowly. The presence of weak catechesis does not mean the tradition is false; it means formation is still needed. The presence of inconsistency does not mean the sacraments are unreal; it means humans are inconsistent. The presence of mediocrity does not mean God is absent; it means God is patient.

Disappointment becomes spiritually dangerous when it turns into contempt. A new convert can begin to despise "the average people in the pew" for being less informed or less passionate. That contempt then poisons parish belonging. It creates loneliness. It turns the convert into a critic rather than a disciple. The irony is that the convert came seeking "the real Church," and now risks refusing the Church where it actually exists: among ordinary people.

4) The difference between a tradition and its local expression

A tradition is more than its best influencers and more than its weakest parishes. A tradition includes doctrine, worship, spiritual practices, pastoral habits, and a history of saints. Any given parish is a local expression of that tradition, shaped by particular clergy, demographics, resources, and cultural pressures.

Online content often collapses these distinctions. It presents "Catholicism" or "Orthodoxy" or "Evangelicalism" as a unified reality. Parish life reveals that local expression varies dramatically. Some parishes are richly catechetical, reverent, and vibrant. Others are struggling. Some are spiritually alive. Others are spiritually thin. That does not invalidate the tradition. It means a person must learn patience, discernment, and realistic expectations.

5) A pastoral warning for converts: do not convert to an influencer

There is a form of "conversion" that is actually attachment to a particular online personality. A person loves the tone, the clarity, the confidence, the community vibe, the aesthetics, the style of worship, the way the tradition is framed. None of that is bad. But it can become a trap if the person is, in practice, converting to an online experience rather than to Christ and the Church.

When that happens, the parish feels like a downgrade. The convert does not find their online community in the pew. They feel lonely. They feel superior or misunderstood. They may bounce from parish to parish trying to find the "real thing" they saw online.

The healthier approach is to convert (or return) with this in mind: **the parish is where you learn love.** It is where you learn patience, service, forgiveness, endurance, and humility. It is where you become part of a Body, not just an audience.

6) Practical guidance for seekers and converts

If you are exploring a tradition largely through online sources:

- **Visit multiple parishes/communities** before drawing conclusions. One parish is not "the tradition."
- **Expect uneven catechesis.** Do not let that surprise you.
- **Bring your hunger for learning—but do not despise others.**

- **Choose rootedness over constant comparison.** Online excellence is not your daily bread; worship and community are.

- **Find one or two real relationships locally** (a pastor, a catechist, a mature believer) rather than assuming the whole parish will match your intensity.

- **Serve.** Service is the quickest path from critique to belonging.

- **Keep learning outside Sunday.** A parish may not provide all the formation you want; that does not mean you cannot pursue it responsibly.

7) Practical guidance for online evangelists and apologists

If you create content that attracts seekers:

- **Name the gap honestly.** Tell people: "Online life is not the parish."

- **Encourage realistic expectations.** Explain that parish communities are mixed and formation varies.

- **Direct people toward local belonging.** Do not let your channel become their "church."

- **Avoid romanticizing.** Do not sell an idealized version of a tradition that most parishes cannot match.

- **Teach converts to love ordinary Christians.** Not everyone will be an apologist. That is okay.

- **Promote formation pathways** (good catechisms, reading plans, local OCIA/formation, spiritual direction).

Online ministry should function like a **signpost**, not a replacement home. It should point people toward embodied worship and local community, not trap them in a perpetual digital apprenticeship.

8) A final word: the real Church is often ordinary

It is tempting to believe that "real Christianity" is always intense, articulate, and aesthetically perfect. But the New Testament tells a different story. The Church is a body of weak members, ordinary believers, imperfect leaders, and slow-growing disciples—held together by grace. The parish is where most saints are made, not because it is glamorous, but because it is ordinary. It is precisely in the ordinary that love becomes real.

The internet can introduce you to a tradition's riches. The parish will introduce you to the tradition's people. You need both. But you must not confuse them.

If your online discovery leads you into a real parish with realistic expectations, you will be less likely to become disillusioned. You will be more likely to become what the internet cannot produce on its own: not merely informed, but faithful—shining with the quiet light of obedience, love, and perseverance.

Discussion Questions

1. What expectations have you formed about a tradition based on online content? Which of those expectations might be unrealistic?

2. Have you ever felt contempt toward "average believers" because their formation was thinner than yours? What would humility and love look like instead?

3. How can online resources serve parish life rather than replace it?

4. If you are a creator: do you present your tradition in a way that prepares people for ordinary parish realities—or do you accidentally sell an ideal?

5. What practical steps could help a seeker move from online learning into embodied community and service?

Chapter 19

Prophetic Voices Online: Truth, Prayer, and the Courage to Name the Idols

The online Christian world needs more than defenders, debaters, and brand-builders. It needs **prophetic voices**—men and women formed by prayer and the tradition, who can speak truthfully about public life without becoming the mouthpiece of any party, empire, or ideology.

That is harder than it sounds. The attention economy rewards hot takes. Political machines reward loyalty. Comment sections reward outrage. And when Christians speak about poverty, war, race, immigration, sexuality, religious liberty, corruption, or the dignity of human life, they are quickly sorted into labels. One famous line—often attributed to Brazil's Archbishop Hélder Câmara—captures the risk: *"When I give food to the poor, they call me a saint. When I ask why they are poor, they call me a communist."*

That is the prophetic dilemma in miniature. **Mercy is applauded when it stays comfortable.** But when mercy becomes truth—when it asks about causes, structures, and idols—someone will accuse it of being "political," "subversive," or "ideological." The prophet learns to live with that cost.

1) Why the prophetic call is costly online

Prophetic speech is rarely rewarded in the short term. It interrupts the comforting stories we tell ourselves. It refuses the easy division of the world into "our righteous tribe" and "their evil tribe." It exposes not only the sins of "the other side," but the sins we protect because they benefit us.

Online, that cost can take predictable forms:

- **Slander and misrepresentation:** People quote-mine, clip, and caricature.

- **Friendly fire:** Fellow Christians treat you as disloyal for refusing tribal scripts.

- **Platform pressure:** Algorithms punish nuance. Sponsors punish controversy. Audiences punish repentance.

- **Spiritual danger:** Prophetic speech can turn into prophetic performance—where "calling out" replaces prayer, humility, and love.

If prophecy is not rooted in worship and accountability, it easily becomes another kind of influence campaign.

2) No political order fully embodies the Gospel

The Church has learned this lesson repeatedly. The Roman Empire did not embody the fullness of the Gospel. Neither did the Byzantine Empire, nor the Holy Roman Empire, nor any modern nation-state. Political orders can sometimes protect goods the Gospel affirms (peace, justice, order, the defense of the vulnerable), but they can also demand allegiance in ways that rival Christ.

This is why Christians must resist a recurring temptation: **civil religion**—the conversion of Christianity into an ideology that blesses the state, sanctifies a tribe, and turns the Cross into a flag.

When political movements capture Christianity, the faith is reduced to a tool:

- a vocabulary for power,
- a justification for enemies,
- a permission slip for contempt,
- a moral badge worn while ignoring inconvenient commands of Jesus.

Prophetic creators are needed precisely here: to remind Christians that **Christ is Lord**, not any party, leader, nation, or cultural project.

3) Prophetic speech must be traditional and loving

A genuine prophetic voice is not merely angry. It is **truthful, prayerful**, and **formed by the Church's moral tradition**. It knows the difference between naming sin and hating sinners. It refuses to dehumanize. It condemns idols without creating new idols.

The prophet therefore speaks in a way that is recognizably Christian:

- **Prayer first:** Scripture commands prayer "for kings and all who are in high positions" (1 Timothy 2:1–2). Prophetic speech that never prays becomes mere activism.
- **Truth with courage:** Sometimes Christians must say, "We must obey God rather than men" (Acts 5:29).
- **Love without surrender:** Love does not mean silence, and truth does not require cruelty.
- **Repentance begins at home:** Prophets call *their own people* to conversion first.

- **Hope, not doom:** Prophets do not merely denounce; they also proclaim God's possibility of repentance, repair, and renewal.

This matters because online ecosystems can form a person into a "prophet" who is actually a partisan priest—someone who baptizes their tribe's instincts and calls it righteousness. The antidote is a deep immersion in the whole counsel of Christian moral teaching: the dignity of every human person, the priority of the poor, the sanctity of life, the demands of peace and justice, the seriousness of truthfulness, and the refusal of hatred.

4) Naming idols without becoming an ideologue

The prophet's central task is to expose false worship. Idols are not only statues; they are ultimate loyalties.

Online, the common idols are familiar:

- **The idol of power:** "If we just win, we can do anything."
- **The idol of tribe:** "My side can do no wrong."
- **The idol of outrage:** "Anger proves I'm faithful."
- **The idol of security:** "Protect comfort at any cost."
- **The idol of money:** "We cannot speak if it costs us."
- **The idol of influence:** "If I lose the platform, I lose my mission."

Prophetic creators must refuse to be captured by these. That does not mean refusing political engagement. It means refusing **ultimate political belonging**—refusing to let politics become the replacement religion, the substitute church, the new liturgy of the feed.

A good test is simple: *Can you criticize the sins of your own side with the same clarity you criticize the other side?* If not, you may not be doing prophecy; you may be doing propaganda.

5) Practical commitments for prophetic content creators

Here are concrete practices that keep prophetic witness Christian rather than merely reactive:

A. Pray publicly for leaders before critiquing them.
Not as a performance, but as a habit that reforms the heart. It reminds your audience that leaders are not demons to be destroyed but persons under God's judgment and mercy.

B. Speak from principles more than party scripts.
Ground claims in Scripture, the virtues, and the tradition's moral reasoning. Avoid adopting the slogans of any movement as if they were the Gospel.

C. Separate diagnosis from demonization.
Name injustice clearly, but refuse contempt. Do not build an audience that bonds through hatred.

D. Refuse "cheap sainthood."
Works of mercy matter. But prophetic love also asks hard questions about why the vulnerable remain vulnerable. Câmara's line is a warning that "being called a saint" can become a way to avoid costly truth.

E. Expect a cost—and decide in advance what you will not trade.
If faithfulness costs followers, will you remain faithful? If it costs sponsorships, will you tell the truth anyway? The prophet plans for the loss so the loss does not control him.

F. Stay accountable and embodied.
Prophetic creators who are not rooted in local worship and real

community often drift into rage or fantasy. The Church is where prophecy is purified.

6) The goal: a new way of being

Christianity is not a political program, but it is also not apolitical. It is a **way of life**—a new way of relating to God and to each other. That way inevitably has public consequences. It forms people who cannot comfortably worship the idols of the age. It creates citizens who can cooperate for the common good but who will not surrender their conscience to the state. It produces servants who feed the poor, and also disciples who ask why poverty persists.

Online, that kind of witness is desperately needed: content creators who will pray, speak, serve, and suffer; who will refuse ideology; who will name idols with tears rather than sneers; and who will keep pointing beyond every earthly power to the Kingdom that no empire can contain.

Discussion Questions

1. Which idol is most likely to capture your online "prophetic" instincts: power, tribe, outrage, security, money, or influence?

2. Can you name injustices and falsehoods without slipping into contempt? What practices help you do that?

3. When you critique leaders or movements, do you also pray for them (1 Timothy 2:1–2)? Why or why not?

4. How can you speak hard truths in a way that invites repentance rather than merely rallies your side?

5. What costs are you willing to bear for faithfulness—and what costs do you fear most?

Closing Prayer

Lord Jesus Christ, you are King of kings, and your Kingdom is not the possession of any empire, party, or movement. Purify my heart from the love of power, the intoxication of outrage, and the comfort of tribal belonging. Teach me to pray for leaders, to speak truth without contempt, and to name the idols of my age with courage and love. Make my life a faithful witness—rooted in worship, accountable in community, and shaped by the Cross—so that my words may serve your people and honor your Name. Amen.

Chapter 20

Conversions, Care, and Responsibility: Receiving Souls Without Triumph

Conversions are occasions for joy. The Church has always rejoiced when a person turns toward Christ, receives baptism, enters communion, or comes home after years away. It is right to give thanks. It is right to celebrate. But in the age of platforms, conversion can easily become something else: **a trophy, a talking point, or content.**

This chapter is a pastoral warning and a set of ethical practices for anyone whose online work influences conversions—especially when those conversions are visible, public, and tied to a creator's identity or "side."

1) Why conversions online require special reverence

A conversion is not merely a change of opinion. It is a human being responding to grace—often through a complex mixture of longing, reasoning, suffering, and hope. Conversions frequently involve vulnerability: leaving familiar communities, risking family tension, rethinking identity, and admitting past error. That vulnerability deserves protection.

Online culture, however, treats everything as shareable. A convert becomes a narrative. Their story becomes proof. Their face becomes marketing. Their former tradition becomes an enemy to repudiate. The convert becomes a symbol used to validate the influencer's brand.

This is spiritually dangerous for the convert and for the community receiving them. It can feed pride, foster resentment, and turn discipleship into performance.

2) Rejoice without parading the person

It is good to celebrate conversion. It is not good to **parade** a convert.

"Parading" happens when the convert is treated as:

- a public badge of victory ("See? We were right.")
- a weapon against others ("Look who left your tradition.")
- an advertising asset ("New episode: ex-[group] destroys their old church!")
- a mascot ("Our newest star; watch their testimony.")

Even when the convert consents, the spiritual risk remains. Early enthusiasm can be mixed with fragility. The convert may not yet understand the pressures of public identity. They may later regret having their story permanently online. Or they may feel trapped in a persona they can't sustain.

A wise content creator protects converts from becoming symbols. They celebrate with gratitude and restraint, keeping the focus on Christ rather than on the win.

3) Reject triumphalist apologetics

Online apologetics can subtly become triumphalist: debates framed as conquest, conversions framed as humiliations, and "wins" used to establish superiority. When that spirit surrounds conversion, it harms everyone:

- It harms the convert by pushing them into a victory narrative rather than a repentance narrative.
- It harms the former community by turning real people into enemies.
- It harms the receiving community by training it to hunger for trophies rather than holiness.
- It harms the influencer by feeding pride and cultivating contempt.

If a conversion is celebrated mainly because it proves "our side" is smarter, purer, or stronger, then the celebration is not Christian. The joy of conversion is joy that someone is nearer to Christ—whether through baptism, communion, renewed faith, or deeper discipleship—not joy that "we beat them."

4) Responsibilities of content creators whose work attracts converts

If your content influences conversions, your responsibility is heavier than you may realize. People may make life-changing decisions based partly on what you model and what you omit.

Here are core responsibilities:

A. Tell the truth about the tradition you represent.
Do not sell an idealized fantasy that local parish life cannot deliver. Do not hide problems. Do not exaggerate strengths. Converts deserve realism.

B. Encourage embodied local processes.
Point converts toward local clergy, catechesis, and community, not toward loyalty to your channel. Your platform should be a signpost, not a substitute parish.

C. Resist turning conversions into content arcs.
Avoid "conversion season" as a growth strategy. Avoid "reaction videos" that frame a convert's former tradition as a punching bag.

D. Protect confidentiality and pacing.
Some conversions should not be public for a long time—sometimes never. Give people permission to stay private.

E. Emphasize ongoing formation.
Conversion is a beginning, not a finish line. Stress prayer, virtue, catechesis, and communal life, not identity-signaling.

5) A special word to creators who themselves are converting

When a content creator converts, the stakes increase. Their audience will interpret the conversion as a signal. The platform will pressure them to narrate every stage, to release reaction content, and to keep the drama moving. But the spiritually healthy path is often the opposite: **slow down.**

If you are converting or changing communions:

Take time off, or significantly reduce output.
Not because conversion is shameful, but because it is sacred and destabilizing. You need space to pray, learn, and be formed without turning your soul into a livestream.

Submit to formation in the new tradition.
Be teachable. Receive catechesis. Learn the worship, the spiritual disciplines, and the moral vision. Let your new community know you personally, beyond your public persona.

Avoid immediate "I was wrong, they were evil" narratives.
Your former tradition may have real problems, but it likely also carried gifts. It is rarely holy to speak as though everything behind you was darkness and everything ahead is light. That tone invites pride and produces unnecessary scandal.

Delay public apologetic combat on behalf of the new tradition.
In the first season after converting, you may not yet understand the tradition's internal debates, pastoral realities, and nuances. Quick triumphal apologetics often reveals immaturity, not conviction.

A mature approach sounds like: "I am entering this tradition with gratitude and humility. I'm still learning. Please pray for me."

6) The warning sign: serial conversions as spectacle

Online audiences often find conversions fascinating, and platforms reward the story. This creates a temptation: some people begin to convert repeatedly, or at least to flirt publicly with new traditions, because it generates attention and a sense of significance. The "journey" becomes the brand.

But frequent conversions can be a symptom of instability rather than discernment. It may indicate:

- restlessness that seeks novelty
- unresolved personal wounds projected onto institutions
- a craving for the adrenaline of reinvention
- a pattern of idealization and disappointment
- an unhealed need to belong that cannot tolerate ordinary imperfection

This does not mean every person who changes communions is unfaithful. Sometimes it is an honest act of conscience. But when the pattern becomes routine and public, it is often a sign that the person is not being formed by a stable rule of life, local community, and accountable discernment.

Christian content creators should be especially cautious here, because their instability can become a spectacle that harms followers—training them to treat the Church like a marketplace and discipleship like a lifestyle swap.

7) How to celebrate conversions faithfully

Here are healthier ways to rejoice without triumph:

- Celebrate Christ's mercy more than your tradition's superiority.
- Keep the convert's identity and story protected unless they insist on sharing and have time to consider consequences.
- If sharing a testimony, focus on grace, prayer, and growth rather than on humiliation of others.
- Encourage the convert to root themselves in a parish and a rule of life before becoming a public spokesperson.
- Keep the tone reverent: conversion is holy ground.

A community that celebrates conversions with reverence becomes a place of healing. A community that celebrates conversions as trophies becomes a place of pride—and pride always collapses.

Discussion Questions

1. When you hear of someone converting to your tradition, what do you feel first: gratitude, excitement, superiority, vindication, or love for the person?
2. Have you ever seen a convert used as "proof" in online apologetics? What did that do to the person and to the audience?

3. If you are a creator: do you subtly rely on conversion stories for momentum and growth? What would faithfulness look like without that incentive?

4. If you have converted (or are converting): what safeguards would help you slow down, learn deeply, and avoid turning the process into content?

5. What signs might indicate that someone is "serial converting" for attention rather than for sustained discipleship?

Closing Prayer

Lord Jesus Christ, Shepherd of souls, thank you for every person you draw toward yourself. Deliver us from triumphalism, from treating conversions as trophies, and from parading vulnerable people for the sake of influence. Give us reverence for persons, patience for formation, and humility in our speech about other communities. Grant converts deep roots in prayer, worship, and local fellowship, and grant content creators wisdom to protect, not exploit, the work of grace. May all our rejoicing be centered on you, who saves and gathers, now and forever. Amen.

Conclusion

The Demand of Discipleship in the Age of Cheap Grace

The digital world offers Christians a strange bargain. It offers visibility without holiness, influence without obedience, audience without communion, and "spiritual content" without the spiritual life. It offers what feels like mission without the cross. And because the attention economy is built on speed and performance, it can make that bargain look normal—even noble. We tell ourselves we are "doing evangelism" because we are posting, debating, and reacting. We tell ourselves we are "defending the faith" because we have gathered supporters and won arguments. We tell ourselves we are "being faithful" because our side applauds us.

But Christ offers no such bargain.

The central question of this book has been simple, and it is the question that will remain when every platform has passed away: **Will we make disciples, or will we gather followers?** Will we pursue faithfulness, or will we pursue influence? Will we love truth and neighbor, or will we build a Christian presence that is powered by outrage, vanity, and money? The age of cheap grace makes it easy to appear Christian without paying the cost of discipleship. Yet the Gospel insists that discipleship costs everything—and that the cost is also the path to life.

Jesus names the demand without apology: "If any man would come after me, let him deny himself and take up his cross daily and follow me" (Luke 9:23, RSV). This is not a suggestion for advanced believers. It is the basic shape of Christian life. It is daily. It is self-denial. It is cross-bearing. And it is following—following Christ rather than following the algorithm, following Christ rather than following the crowd, following Christ rather than following our own need to be seen.

Luke's next lines make the cost even clearer: "For whoever would save his life will lose it; and whoever loses his life for my sake, he will save it. For what does it profit a man if he gains the whole world and loses or forfeits himself?" (Luke 9:24–25, RSV). The platform constantly promises profit: growth, reach, recognition. It invites us to "gain the world" in small digital forms—likes, shares, subscriber counts, the thrill of being known. But Jesus asks a deeper question: what will it profit you if you gain influence and lose yourself? If you build an online ministry and become angry, harsh, vain, and unfree—what have you gained?

This is why the temptation of cheap grace is so dangerous online. Cheap grace is grace without the cross, forgiveness without repentance, comfort without conversion, Christianity as identity without Christianity as obedience. It is the kind of religion that allows a person to feel safe while staying unchanged. And because platforms reward performance, cheap grace can look like a thriving "ministry." But Jesus says discipleship is the way of the cross. If there is no cross—no repentance, no humility, no obedience, no love—then what we are building is not discipleship. It is imitation.

The rich young man and the price of letting go

Mark tells us about a man who runs to Jesus with sincere urgency: "Good Teacher, what must I do to inherit eternal life?" (Mark 10:17,

RSV). He is not hostile. He is searching. He has moral seriousness. When Jesus calls him to the commandments, he replies, "Teacher, all these I have observed from my youth" (Mark 10:20). Then comes one of the most revealing sentences in the Gospels: "And Jesus looking upon him loved him" (Mark 10:21). Christ's demand is not born from contempt. It is born from love.

Yet love does not mean lowering the standard. Jesus says, "You lack one thing; go, sell what you have… and come, follow me" (Mark 10:21). The man's response is heartbreaking: "His countenance fell, and he went away sorrowful; for he had great possessions" (Mark 10:22). He wants eternal life, but he cannot let go.

In the age of online influence, "possessions" are not only money. They can be reputation, audience, platform access, the approval of a tribe, the comfort of being praised, the security of a brand. Jesus' question to the rich young man becomes a question to every Christian influencer: **What are you unwilling to surrender?** Would you lose subscribers to remain truthful? Would you lose influence to remain charitable? Would you let your platform shrink if Christ were served better by your obscurity? Would you stop posting a profitable kind of content if it was deforming your soul? Would you step away from a controversy if engaging would train your audience toward contempt?

Jesus loved the rich young man enough to demand freedom. And the demand is the same for us. Christ does not call us merely to keep religious habits while clinging to what owns us. He calls us to follow. Online discipleship becomes real only when we are willing to let go of what holds our hearts captive—whether that is money, attention, or applause.

The dishonest steward and the question of masters

Luke gives another parable that speaks sharply to the age of monetized ministry: the parable of the dishonest steward (Luke 16:1–13). The steward is accused of wasting his master's goods, and he responds with shrewdness to protect his future. Jesus' teaching here is challenging, but the parable ends with a clear moral boundary: "No servant can serve two masters... You cannot serve God and mammon" (Luke 16:13, RSV).

Online ministry constantly tempts us to serve two masters. We try to serve Christ and the algorithm. We try to serve Christ and our brand. We try to serve Christ and donor expectations. We try to serve Christ and the applause of our "side." But Jesus says it cannot be done. Not forever. Eventually one master will win.

The question is not only whether we preach true things. The question is what governs us. If the fear of losing income controls your speech, money is your master. If the fear of losing relevance controls your speech, influence is your master. If the hunger for applause controls your speech, the crowd is your master. And if Christ is not your master, then even religious content becomes a form of misdirection—because it is not ordered toward obedience.

Jesus' warning is therefore an act of mercy. He is freeing us from double-mindedness. He is calling us back to a simple allegiance: serve God.

The cross as the measure of online faithfulness

Throughout this book we have returned, again and again, to a consistent biblical pattern: God measures faithfulness differently than platforms do. Platforms measure success by visibility, engagement, and growth. Christ measures faithfulness by obedience, love, humility, truth, and perseverance. Platforms train us to be reactive and tribal. Christ trains us to be reverent, patient, and charitable. Platforms invite us to build cults of personality. John the Baptist teaches us to decrease. Platforms reward contempt. Jesus warns that contempt endangers the soul. Platforms invite us to overexpose holy things. Scripture calls us stewards of mysteries. Platforms offer cheap grace. Jesus offers the cross.

The demand of discipleship is therefore the demand to live as Christians online in the same way we are called to live as Christians everywhere: as people under authority, committed to prayer, formed by truth, devoted to love, and willing to suffer rather than to sin. It is the demand to practice what we proclaim. It is the demand to choose the good of the other over the pleasure of the dunk. It is the demand to remember the person behind the screen. It is the demand to speak in ways that heal. It is the demand to be light.

And it is, above all, the demand to follow Christ.

Luke's words press the point to the end: "For whoever is ashamed of me and of my words, of him will the Son of man be ashamed when he comes in his glory" (Luke 9:26, RSV). Online life tempts Christians to be ashamed in subtle ways—not by denying Christ explicitly, but by reshaping him into a more marketable figure. We soften hard truths to keep followers. We adopt harshness to keep attention. We make the Gospel entertaining so it will sell. We present Christianity as a lifestyle brand rather than as repentance and new life. That is a form of shame, because it treats Christ's words as negotiable.

The way forward is not fear. It is clarity. Christ calls you to himself. He calls you to daily obedience. He calls you to carry the cross, not because he delights in your suffering, but because the cross is the path through which self-worship dies and love becomes real. He calls you to be free of what owns you. He calls you to serve God rather than mammon. He calls you to become a disciple who makes disciples.

A final invitation

If you are reading this as a Christian creator or would-be evangelist, the call is not to be perfect before you begin. The call is to be honest about what you are doing and who you are serving. Begin with prayer. Receive correction. Tell the truth. Love your neighbor. Set boundaries. Resist contempt. Seek holiness. And when you fail, repent quickly—because repentance is not the end of ministry; it is the heart of it.

If you are reading this as a viewer, supporter, or follower of Christian content, the call is equally urgent: do not settle for cheap grace. Do not substitute consumption for obedience. Do not confuse admiration for discipleship. Follow Christ in your actual life. Join a community. Serve your neighbor. Pray. Repent. Take up your cross. Become the light you are meant to be.

The platforms will change. The algorithms will shift. Fame will fade. But the demand of discipleship will remain, because the Lord remains.

"He who loses his life for my sake... will save it" (Luke 9:24). That is the promise that breaks the bargain of cheap grace. That is the hope that makes faithfulness possible. And that is the freedom that allows Christians, even in the attention economy, to choose Christ over influence—every day.

Discussion Questions

1. What "possessions" (Mark 10:22) are hardest for you to surrender in digital ministry—approval, comfort, income, control, reputation, or something else?

2. In what ways are you tempted to serve two masters (Luke 16:13)—Christ and money, Christ and the crowd, Christ and the algorithm?

3. What does it look like for you to "take up your cross daily" (Luke 9:23) in the concrete practices of online speech—truthfulness, charity, restraint, humility, prayer?

4. Where might you be living in "cheap grace"—talking about faith more than practicing obedience, consuming content more than doing the word?

5. If your platform disappeared tomorrow, what would remain of your discipleship and mission? What does your answer reveal?

Closing Prayer

Lord Jesus Christ, you have called us not to cheap grace but to the way of the cross. Deliver me from the desire to gain the world while losing myself. Free me from whatever I cling to more than you—money, influence, applause, or comfort. Teach me to deny myself, take up my cross daily, and follow you with joy. Give me courage to choose faithfulness over visibility and obedience over success. Make me a true disciple who helps others become disciples, for you are Lord, and you alone are worthy. Amen.

Appendix A

A Discernment Worksheet: "Should I Post This?"

Use this worksheet as a **pause button** before you publish—especially when you feel urgent, angry, excited, or afraid. You can print it, keep it near your desk, or copy it into a notes app. The goal is not perfection. The goal is **faithfulness**.

---

1) Name the Moment

What am I about to post? (one sentence)

Why now?

- ☐ I feel urgency
- ☐ I feel anger / indignation
- ☐ I feel anxiety / fear
- ☐ I feel excitement / "this will do well"
- ☐ I feel grief
- ☐ I feel compassion
- ☐ Other: _____

If I wait 24 hours, what might improve?

2) Check the Heart

My main motive is... (circle one)
Witness / Help / Teach / Warn / Clarify / Defend / Vent / Win / Be seen / Be praised / Get even

Am I seeking discipleship outcomes or engagement outcomes?

- ☐ Discipleship
- ☐ Engagement
- ☐ Honestly: both
- ☐ Unsure

Is there any "beam" in my eye right now? (pride, contempt, envy, fear, vanity, impatience)

_____

_____

3) Pray Before You Publish

Pause for one minute.

Brief prayer: "Lord, purify my motives, guard my tongue, and let this serve your truth and love."

After praying, do I still feel compelled to post?

- ☐ Yes, with peace
- ☐ Yes, but I'm still heated
- ☐ No, I should wait
- ☐ Unsure

4) Truthfulness and Verification

What exactly am I claiming? (list the key assertions)

1. _____
2. _____
3. _____

What is my evidence?

- ☐ Primary source (full context)
- ☐ Multiple reputable sources
- ☐ One source
- ☐ A clip/screenshot without full context
- ☐ A rumor / "people are saying"
- ☐ I'm not sure

Have I read/watched the original in full?

- ☐ Yes
- ☐ No
- ☐ Not possible

Am I being fair to the other view/person?

- ☐ I can state their position in a way they would recognize
- ☐ I'm probably oversimplifying
- ☐ I'm reacting to a caricature

If I'm wrong, what harm could this cause?

_____

5) Charity and Tone

Would I say this the same way face-to-face with a real person present?

- ☐ Yes
- ☐ No
- ☐ Not sure

Does my tone contain contempt?
("You fool," mockery, sneering, dehumanizing labels, delight in humiliation)

- ☐ No
- ☐ A little
- ☐ Honestly, yes

Am I correcting as a physician or performing as an executioner?

- ☐ Physician (aiming at repentance/healing)
- ☐ Executioner (aiming at punishment/humiliation)
- ☐ Mixed

Rewrite one sentence to remove heat and increase clarity:
Before: _____
After: _____

---

6) The Person Behind the Screen

Who could be harmed by this post?

- ☐ The person I'm discussing

- ☐ Their family / minors
- ☐ Vulnerable viewers (trauma, scrupulosity, anxiety)
- ☐ My own soul (anger, pride, obsession)
- ☐ The Church's witness
- ☐ Other: _____

Am I treating anyone as disposable?

- ☐ No
- ☐ Possibly
- ☐ Yes

Have I prayed for the person/group I'm addressing?

- ☐ Yes
- ☐ Not yet

---

7) Scandal, Stewardship, and "Pearls"

Is this content about something holy, private, or easily mocked?

- ☐ No
- ☐ Yes (explain): _____

Am I overexposing something that needs reverent reserve? (confessional-style issues, private pastoral matters, vulnerable people, sacred practices)

- ☐ No
- ☐ Possibly

- ☐ Yes

Is this the right stage for the audience I have?

- ☐ Intro level
- ☐ Intermediate
- ☐ Advanced
- ☐ Mixed audience—high risk of misunderstanding

---

8) Authority and Accountability

Have I run this by anyone who can correct me?

- ☐ Pastor / spiritual director
- ☐ Trusted peer / accountability partner
- ☐ Moderator/team
- ☐ No

If I won't show it to anyone wise, why?

---

9) Money, Metrics, and Hidden Incentives

Would I still post this if it got very little engagement?

- ☐ Yes
- ☐ No
- ☐ Not sure

Would I still post this if it cost me followers/supporters?

- ☐ Yes
- ☐ No
- ☐ Not sure

Am I posting because it is "what my audience wants"?

- ☐ No
- ☐ Somewhat
- ☐ Yes

---

10) The "Cross Test"

Does this post reflect self-denial and obedience, or self-display and control?

- ☐ Obedience
- ☐ Self-display
- ☐ Mixed

Is there a quieter, more faithful alternative?

- ☐ Pray instead
- ☐ Message privately instead of posting publicly
- ☐ Ask a question rather than make an accusation
- ☐ Share Scripture and a practice rather than hot commentary
- ☐ Wait 24–72 hours
- ☐ Don't post at all

11) Decision

Choose one:

- ☐ **Post now** (peaceful, verified, charitable, necessary)
- ☐ **Revise and post later** (tone/clarity needs work)
- ☐ **Seek counsel first** (authority/accountability needed)
- ☐ **Move it to a private conversation** (pastoral sensitivity)
- ☐ **Do not post** (would harm, inflate, or scandalize)

My decision and why (two sentences):

_____
_____
_____

12) After-Action Review (Use 24–72 hours later)

What fruit did this produce?

- ☐ Clarity
- ☐ Peace
- ☐ Repentance
- ☐ Greater charity
- ☐ Confusion
- ☐ Rage/pile-on
- ☐ Pride in me
- ☐ Shame in others
- ☐ Other: _____

What would I do differently next time?

One closing sentence-prayer:

"Lord, keep me faithful—truthful, charitable, and free—so my words may serve your discipleship."

Appendix B

Internal Handbook for Christian Content Creators

How to practice ethical digital mission with examples, templates, and procedures.

This handbook turns the public Code of Ethics into **workable internal policies**. Adapt it to your tradition, team size, and platform mix. When in doubt: choose what best serves **truth, charity, holiness, and the protection of souls**.

---

1) Mission and Operating Principles

1.1 Mission statement (internal)

We exist to help people become disciples of Jesus Christ, not merely followers of our channel. Our content aims at **truth, prayer, holiness, and love,** with an emphasis on embodied Christian life in local community.

1.2 The non-negotiables

We will not:

- Spread unverified claims or "rumor content."
- Build audiences through contempt, mockery, or pile-ons.

- Monetize in a way that manipulates donors or creates spiritual dependence.
- Expose private/pastoral/confessional material for content.
- Function as a substitute church through DMs.

1.3 The internal "Cross Test"

Before any major post, ask:
Does this reflect self-denial and obedience (Luke 9:23), or self-display and control?
If it's mainly self-display, we pause.

---

2) Truthfulness and Citations Policy

2.1 Definitions

- **Primary source:** the original sermon, document, full interview, full article, official statement, or direct data.
- **Secondary source:** commentary or summaries by others.
- **Claim types:**
    - *Fact claim* ("X happened," "Y said Z," "the policy states…")
    - *Interpretation* ("This suggests…," "I think this means…")
    - *Pastoral judgment* ("This could scandalize…," "This may harm…")

2.2 Verification standards

We do not publish fact claims unless one of these is true:

1. We have the primary source in full context, or

2. Two independent reputable sources corroborate, or
3. We state clearly: "This is unconfirmed / developing," and we treat it with restraint (often: we don't post at all).

We do not publish accusations (of abuse, fraud, criminality, etc.) without primary documentation or robust, reputable reporting—and even then we use pastoral caution.

2.3 Citation practices by platform

Video (YouTube)

- Put sources in the description under "Sources."
- Use on-screen lower third for key citations when feasible.
- If quoting, show the quote and reference.
- If summarizing, link the source and state that it's a summary.

Example (YouTube description):

Sources:

1. "Title of document/interview," Publisher/Host, date (link)
2. Official statement from ____ (link)
3. Scholarly article/book reference: Author, Title, page #

Short-form (TikTok/IG Reels)

- Use a pinned comment with sources.
- If you can't cite due to format limits, either:
    - Keep claims general and non-accusatory, or
    - Point to a longer version with full sources.

Example pinned comment:

Sources for this clip: [link to statement], [link to full talk], [link to data]. Full context in bio.

Written posts (blog/newsletter)

- Use footnotes or endnotes.
- Quote in context; avoid quote-mining.

2.4 Quote integrity rules

- Never alter a quote's meaning through ellipses.
- Always keep enough context to avoid misrepresentation.
- For Scripture, use the same translation consistently (unless explicitly discussing translation differences).

---

3) Corrections and Retractions Procedure

3.1 Correction levels

Level 1: Minor (typos, minor misstatement with no meaningful harm)
Level 2: Substantive (incorrect fact, misleading framing, missing context)
Level 3: Serious (false accusation, misidentification, harm to a person/group, privacy breach)

3.2 Correction timeline

- **Level 2–3:** correct within **24–72 hours**, sooner if harm is ongoing.
- If you need time to verify, post: "We are reviewing and will update by [date]."

3.3 Where corrections must appear

Corrections must show up **where the error spread**:

- Video: pinned comment + description update + (if serious) follow-up short.
- Post: edit with timestamped correction note at top or bottom.
- Newsletter: send a correction note in the next edition (or immediate email if serious).

3.4 Correction template (plain and trustworthy)

Template A (standard):

Correction (Date): In my earlier post/video, I said **[specific claim]**. That was incorrect/misleading. The accurate information is **[correct claim]**, supported by **[source]**. I'm sorry for the error and any confusion it caused.

Template B (harm occurred):

Correction and Apology (Date): I misrepresented **[person/group]** when I said **[claim]**. That was wrong. The truth is **[correct claim]**. I apologize to **[person/group]** and to viewers who were misled. I'm taking steps to prevent this, including **[process change]**.

3.5 When to retract (not just correct)

Retract when:

- The central premise was wrong.
- The post creates ongoing reputational harm.
- The content relies on unverified allegations.

Retraction template:

Retraction (Date): I'm removing this post/video because it contains unverified or incorrect claims and may cause harm. I do not stand by it. A corrected summary of what we can responsibly say is **[brief]**, with sources here: **[links]**.

---

4) Conflicts and Controversy Policy

4.1 Steel-man rule

Before critique, ensure we can state the other view in a way they'd recognize as fair.

Internal test:
"Could a thoughtful representative of this view say, 'Yes, that's what we believe'?"

4.2 Avoid "built to dunk" content

We don't publish:

- Mockery compilations
- "Gotcha" edits
- Rage-bait response chains
- Content that exists mainly to humiliate

4.3 Heat protocol (when emotions are high)

If you feel heated:

1. Wait 12–24 hours
2. Pray and re-read
3. Ask a peer reviewer to check tone and fairness
4. If still necessary, publish a calmer version

4.4 Public dispute policy

When conflict involves identifiable individuals:

- Prefer **private contact** first, when appropriate and safe.
- If public response is necessary, speak to:
    - the issue,
    - the principles,
    - and the path forward,
    without doxxing or humiliating.

---

5) Money, Patronage, and Sponsorship Ethics

5.1 Basic commitments

- The Gospel is not for sale.
- Giving must be **free, not coerced**.
- Donors do not control content.
- Financial disclosures are normal, not shameful.

5.2 Monetization types and rules

Donations / Patreon / Membership

Allowed if:

- Benefits are non-pastoral (early access, bonus Q&A, behind-the-scenes).
- No "pay for counsel," "pay for prayer," or "pay for absolution-style" dynamics.
- No spiritual ranking for donors.

Language we avoid:

- "If you really care, you'll give."

- "If we don't hit this goal, truth will be silenced."
- "Don't let the enemies win—donate now."

Language we use:

- "Support is optional. Please prioritize your local church and obligations."
- "Here's what support funds: [equipment/time/charity]."
- "No one is less faithful if they cannot give."

Sponsorships

We disclose clearly at the beginning and in the description.

Verbal disclosure examples:

- "This video is sponsored by ____. They did not review the content, and the views are my own."
- "This link is an affiliate link—at no extra cost to you, it helps support the work."

Sponsorship refusal criteria
We refuse sponsors that:

- Pressure theological compromise
- Require controversy farming
- Create scandal (e.g., predatory products, deceptive claims)
- Conflict with Christian moral commitments

5.3 Financial transparency practice (by size)

Solo creator (small):

- Publish a short annual note: "Support funds X/Y/Z."
- Keep separate bank account if feasible.

Team/ministry (medium+):

- Basic budget categories
- Board/oversight
- Annual report
- Clear policy on salaries, reimbursements, and charity pass-through

---

6) Privacy, Boundaries, and Safeguarding

6.1 Privacy rules

We do not publish:

- minors' identities or locations
- private emails/DMs without consent
- medical details or trauma stories that aren't ours
- screenshots that expose usernames unless necessary and ethically justified

Consent standard: explicit, informed, and revocable.

6.2 "Confession-like DM" policy

We do not perform quasi-sacramental counseling via DMs.

Standard DM response template:

Thank you for trusting me. I'm not able to provide pastoral care through DMs. If you're in danger or considering self-harm, please contact emergency services right now. Otherwise, I strongly encourage you to speak with a local pastor/priest or a qualified counselor. If you tell me your general location, I can suggest how to find a local church/community.

(Adjust for your tradition and safeguarding needs.)

6.3 Parasocial dependence safeguards

Signs of dependence:

- "You're my only spiritual support."
- "I can't trust anyone else."
- constant crisis DMs
- boundary pushing, emotional enmeshment

Response:

- reinforce boundaries
- redirect to local support
- if needed: limit or end contact

---

7) Moderation and Community Standards

7.1 Public comment rules

We remove or block:

- slurs, dehumanization, harassment
- threats
- doxxing
- sexual content involving minors
- repeated bad-faith provocation
- encouragement of self-harm or violence

We discourage:

- dunking and pile-ons
- factional name-calling ("heretics," "idiots," etc.)
- conspiracy-spreading without sources

7.2 Moderation workflow (simple)

1. **Auto filters** for profanity/slurs
2. **First offense:** remove + warn
3. **Second offense:** timeout/mute
4. **Third offense:** block

7.3 "Do not send the mob" policy

If a video/post highlights a harmful idea, we:

- avoid identifying private individuals
- explicitly say: "Do not harass anyone"
- moderate aggressively if pile-ons begin

---

8) Authority, Accountability, and Review

8.1 Accountability structure options

Pick one (or combine):

- Spiritual director or pastor check-in monthly
- Peer review council (2–4 trusted Christians)
- Editorial reviewer for factual and tone checks
- Board/elders if formal ministry

8.2 Review triggers (mandatory review before posting)

- Allegations against individuals or ministries
- Sensitive moral topics likely to inflame
- Money appeals
- Hot controversies with incomplete info
- Content involving vulnerable groups

9) Practical Templates Library

9.1 Source checklist (pre-publication)

- Primary source seen in full
- Quotes verified and contextual
- Opponent view fairly summarized
- Claims separated from interpretation
- Scripture citations accurate
- Links added / bibliography included

9.2 Sponsorship disclosure (copy/paste)

On-screen/voice:

"Sponsored by ____. They did not review this content; the views are my own."

Description:

"Sponsor: ____. Affiliate links may earn a commission at no extra cost. Support is optional."

9.3 Correction note (copy/paste)

Correction (Date): I previously stated ____. That was inaccurate. The correct information is ____, supported by ____. I apologize for the error.

9.4 Conflict-of-interest disclosure (copy/paste)

"Disclosure: I have a relationship with ____ (e.g., I previously worked with them / received a stipend / belong to this community)."

9.5 Comment pin (prevent pile-on)

"Reminder: address ideas, not people. No harassment, insults, or dogpiling. Violations will be removed."

---

10) Examples: Applying the Handbook

Example A: A viral clip of a pastor "saying something outrageous"

Wrong approach: react immediately; quote a 12-second clip; condemn; unleash comments.
Right approach:

1. Find full sermon/interview (primary source)
2. Verify context and exact words
3. Decide if response is necessary
4. If responding, steel-man and correct with restraint
5. Pin "no harassment" comment

Example B: A meme claim ("This council/saint/translation proves…")

Right approach:

- If you can't cite the original source, don't present it as fact.
- Reframe: "I've seen this claim; I'm looking for the primary source. If you have it, send it."

Example C: Donor pressure ("If you don't call out X, I'm canceling support")

Right approach:

- Thank them
- Reaffirm mission
- Refuse donor control
- If needed, let support go

Suggested reply:

"I appreciate your support. I can't shape content around donor demands. I will act according to conscience, truthfulness, and pastoral wisdom."

---

11) Adoption and Review

11.1 Internal onboarding

- Every team member reads this handbook.
- Everyone signs a simple acknowledgement: "I will follow these practices."

11.2 Quarterly ethics review

- Review major posts for: truthfulness, tone, correction speed, donor transparency, moderation health.
- Update policies based on failures and lessons learned.

Made in the USA
Coppell, TX
31 December 2025

67653448R20105